TREELIKE

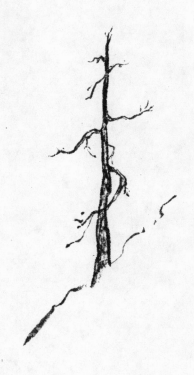

Oakland University
Asian Poetry in Translation: Japan #4

University of Michigan
Michigan Papers in Japanese Studies #8

UNESCO COLLECTION OF REPRESENTATIVE WORKS
JAPANESE SERIES

This work has been accepted in the Japanese Series of
the Translations Collection of the United Nations Edu-
cational, Scientific and Cultural Organization (UNESCO)

This translation of the poetry of Kinoshita Yūji has been
awarded the Japan-United States Friendship Commis-
sion's FRIENDSHIP FUND PRIZE FOR JAPANESE LIT-
ERARY TRANSLATION

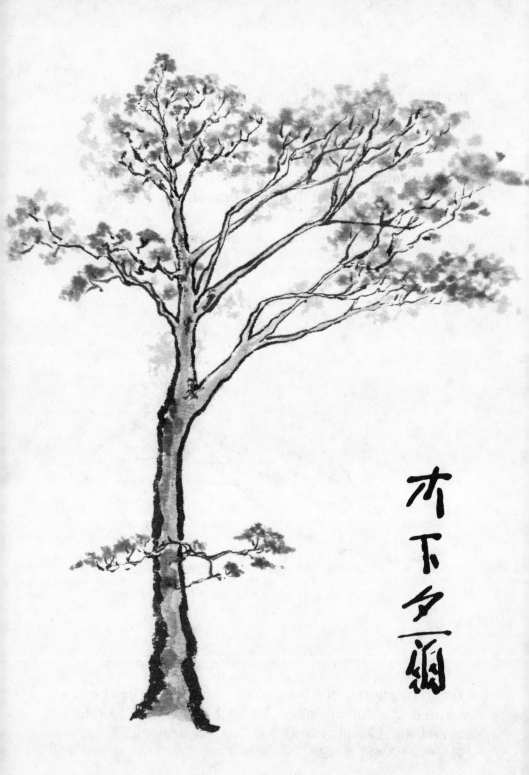

木下夕爾

TREELIKE

The poetry of
KINOSHITA YŪJI

Translated by
ROBERT EPP

Preface by Ōoka Makoto

Published in association with
the Center for Japanese Studies
University of Michigan

Oakland University
KATYDID BOOKS   ROCHESTER, MI   1982

Library of Congress Catalog Card Number: 82-81181
ISBN 0-942668-04-9

First Edition

Sumi-è illustrations by Karen Hargreaves-Fitzsimmons

Printed in the United States of America

ASIAN POETRY IN TRANSLATION is edited by and published under the direction of Thomas Fitzsimmons.

MICHIGAN PAPERS IN JAPANESE STUDIES is published under the direction of John Campbell.

The Japanese text of Kinoshita Yūji's poems is taken from the collection published in 1966 by BOKUYŌSHA, Tokyo, and is reproduced here with the permission of the publisher.

KINOSHITA YŪJI, a critical study by Robert Epp, is available in the TWAYNE WORLD AUTHORS SERIES.

CONTENTS

Poem titles followed by an asterisk refer the reader to a Note in Appendix III.

INTRODUCTORY

These translations are for my mother.

PREFACE

Since the Meiji Restoration more than a century ago, a radical move-
ment for modernization through Europeanization has affected every part
of Japan. To most effectively implement this movement, a centralized
political system led by a powerful bureaucracy was established in
Tokyo—which then became not only the center of political power but
also of cultural development.

Tokyo's influence in education, journalism, publishing, art grew until it
came to be seen as "Chūō" (the Center), a term that suggests its
privileged superiority vis-a-vis the provinces. Painters, composers, nov-
elists, poets born outside Tokyo dreamed, and still do, of settling in the
capital to attain distinction. That Tokyo was in some sense an enormous
window onto the civilization and cultures of Europe and America was an
important aspect of its magnetism.

European-style centralization plus the cult of Western ways made of
Tokyo a dreamland for successive generations of ambitious intellectuals
and artists who then, in this country of little space and many people,
became models for others trying to adjust or conform to life in the
centralized system.

Kinoshita Yūji was born in a small provincial town in Western Japan,
and save for a few years as a student in Tokyo and Nagoya he lived most of
his life in his native place—a fact important to remember when reading
his poems. He very much wanted to settle in Tokyo, but he could not.

Like many poets of his time, Kinoshita was an eager reader of modern
European poetry in translation. Yet his own work remains rooted in the
details of everyday life in the small country town of Hiroshima Prefecture
where he was born. There, as the surviving son responsible for the care of
family and family affairs, he passed a succession of what sometimes
seemed to him monotonous years. But all through those years his keen
gaze fastened on and followed the movement and changes about him as
well as in his own sensibility. Untouched by the trends in Tokyo, he could
from a fresh angle catch and fix in words the shifts of wind and cloud, the
habits of small animals, the afternoon feeling of a small station where no
one boards or descends from the train, passing encounters with people of
the village, a field of withered grass, Japanese vegetables solid on a table,
the shape of cakes made from wild fruit.

In his poems, man and nature live in sympathy. And from that sense of natural harmony he wrote, also, beautiful poems for children.

Kinoshita's poems preserve a natural breath and a tranquility that were already in his time disappearing from Japanese big-city life. Rather than resorting to exaggeration or large-gestured confessions of the modern artist's sense of alienation and the absurd, he worked with firm will to rescue and immortalize the momentary reality of the precious things and events that surrounded him. It is a focus and a will that he shares with the ancient masters of traditional Japanese waka and haikai (haiku). Living in "Chihō" (the Province), far from "Chūō" (the Center) he was able to revive in his own quietly modern way a vocation that had been maintained through the centuries by the poets of old.

And indeed Kinoshita was well known as a haiku poet. The high techniques of crystalization and focus he developed in the practice of that art emerge in his modern verse as a charm of ellipse and suggestiveness, an elegance of simplicity. For this country poet is an elegant poet, one who makes from contemporary Japanese language a very finely textured weaving.

Kinoshita has been fortunate in his translator. Robert Epp's dedication to this work over the past decade seems also to reflect some older, more finely-tuned tradition. Whether in Japan visiting the poet's family and colleagues, eating the regional foods Kinoshita mentions, discussing the poems, the translations (Thomas Fitzsimmons remembers a first phone call from him nine years ago in Tokyo and a whole afternoon of discussion in a coffee shop, and over the years an increasing flow of manuscript), or in Los Angeles revising, sometimes 70 or 80 times and still not being entirely satisfied, Epp's firm will seems to have matched the poet's own. That in the end the translations were satisfactory is attested to by the honors the book already has received.

So there is harmony here between the ways of poet and translator, maker and re-maker. I cannot help but think Kinoshita Yūji would be, is, pleased.

Ōoka Makoto

Tokyo, 1982

TRANSLATOR'S INTRODUCTION

A pharmacist by default, Kinoshita earned his livelihood by filling prescriptions. The premature death of his stepfather in 1935 forced him to take over the family apothecary in his native village of Miyuki, situated near the eastern edge of Hiroshima Prefecture and now incorporated into the city of Fukuyama. This obliged him to transfer from the preparatory course in French literature at Waseda Academy in Tokyo to the School of Pharmacy in Nagoya. He never completely recovered from this crushing of his boyhood dreams.

Although Kinoshita attempted to make filling prescriptions bearable by filling himself with poetry, the two did not mix well. Sometimes, his mind on poetry, he lost track of what ingredients he had included in a mixture and had to throw away the batch and begin anew. In one memorable incident, uncertain of the amount of a potentially lethal drug he had used, he worried whether the patient might die and he himself lose his license; fortunately, neither occurred. When he was not wasting chemicals or misfilling prescriptions, Kinoshita was fond either of leaving on unannounced one-day trips to the mountains or the sea, or of sleeping after a night of poetry till mid-morning. Either way, the business suffered.

Let it suffer! He found the very thought of mixing chemicals abhorrent, the more so if the object was profit. And so, day after day, year in and year out, he exercised his art as Dylan Thomas wrote, "in the still night / When only the moon rages." Or, when he could, in places far removed from the apothecary. Once he even tried to pretend his profession was an art by comparing the pharmacist's sensitivity to the moment when a mixture was "just right" with the poet's sensitivity to the moment when a poem was "just right." But he could neither "poetize" a profession he despised nor associate with those who practiced it. Indeed, he went out of his way to avoid all druggists and gladly suffered fines rather than attend their regular meetings. He lived by pharmacy; he lived for poetry.

His writing brought him local fame and that forced him to shoulder many tasks that interfered with his work. He acquired a following as a haiku teacher, became editorially involved with modern poetry journals, was asked to speak on radio and write texts for school or company songs, was swamped by aspiring poets wanting help with their work, and was talked into writing a series of poems for an illustrated brochure celebrating the 1962 centennial of

Japan National Railways. Such requests depleted his limited physical resources but did not help him feel he had achieved his goals. They did at least involve him directly in poetry, forcing him to challenge inspiration in trying times. His last poem, "Gone So Long," which he wrote as he lay dying of cancer, was requested by a regional newspaper.

*

Returning to Miyuki village deeply affected Kinoshita. Explaining to a friend why he had to drop out of Waseda Academy, he wept openly. His brother claimed that something in him had dried up when he surrendered his hopes of being a professional poet in Tokyo. In particular he lost his capacity for humor. And with good reason. As he states in "Country Table," the title poem of his first collection, he feared he would simmer on a stove in Miyuki for the rest of his days, ultimately "sacrificed" to rural life. He saw himself leading a totally meaningless existence there, growing old in the provinces like "a horsefly buzzing forever near a shiny coil." But, certain he was destined to be a poet, he made up his mind to be one though it meant resigning himself to work at it part time and to write about his country life only.

Kinoshita knew perfectly well that he could not write authentically about city life unless he lived there. The basic dictum of his aesthetic was that a poet remain close to everyday experience if he hopes to write convincing verse. As circumstances dictated that he remain in the country, so his aesthetic dictated that he write about reed flutes and grazing goats rather than about raunchy drunks and traffic jams. Using rustic imagery in itself, however, did not falsify or distort Kinoshita's expression of his deepest, most authentic self, his "so slender griefs" and "private sorrows." It merely clothed his insights and his way of describing grief in different dress. The challenge constantly facing him was how to use natural imagery to reveal rather than veil his despair.

Return to Miyuki village altered the basic nature of Kinoshita's verse. Before 1935 he could only imagine what it meant to be an alienated poet. After 1935, he knew the bitterness of failed dreams, lost hopes, meaningless existence. He was genuinely estranged and lived only for what "goes sparkling off from . . . [his] innermost self," squeezing his writing into the midnight hours. But had pharmacy not compelled him to seek consolation in poetry, he may never have been moved to fashion out of rural images his poignant descriptions of loneliness and lost dreams. When he asks us to "Think of wind's roar that wakes you late at night / as my song / consider it my broken flute," we may wonder what the deepening tone and power of his poetry might owe to the broken flute he played on—the flute that according to Apollinaire is the poet's deepest inner self.

Challenged to describe pain and estrangement in rural images and traditional moods, Kinoshita was compelled to reexplore his native region and its poetic conventions. To creatively exploit his predicament, he had to forge a sense of continuity between past and future, between his rural identity and his alienation. At his late-night desk he explored passageways linking these two aspects of his being and addressed the incongruities of his life: dissonances between rural and urban, between traditional and modern, between what he was and what he wanted to be. In the evenings, his "ears drawn toward the flow of sap," he sat on the mats in his study, a lantern flickering at his elbow, and, as he tells us, calmly lit "private fires to my mind / to the dry grasses in my mind."

A portion of the dry grass was a sense of utter aloneness. Despite growing local appreciation of his work, he felt unloved and regarded himself a failure. He could not be satisfied with acclaim as a regional poet, a "hometown bard." He yearned to be accepted as a modern poet and that, he felt, could be best accomplished in Tokyo. And so the lament that he has passed through life asleep in the countryside, "an infant in a buggy with the hood down." Sensing that he was "the last star to shine," too late in developing a more openly confessional style, he confesses at the end of his life: "Cherishing what bird songs remain / I speak my words in deep shade / a lone tree loath to merge with dusk."

The imagery emerging from Kinoshita's quest forcefully catches the tensions that dominated his life. The very dissonances that affected his existence in Miyuki constitute an important feature of his craft. He enhanced his art by "modernizing" the traditional strain in his work while simultaneously "traditionalizing" the strain that sought to be modern. The traditional aspect frequently suggests the promise of growth or dynamic potential. He can see the future latent in the stubby horns of a tethered calf, the possibilities of shared love in a bird's nest, the kinetic relationship between thought and action in the process of milling grain. Such purely natural imagery, however, often suggests frustrated potential or the static boredom of the country—aspects of Kinoshita's "modern" sensibility.

Typical interplay of such imagery occurs in a 1949 poem. Kinoshita had just missed the train at a small rural station; he will have to wait some time for the next one. The powerful aromas of a ripening citron tree resonate with his customarily acerbic feelings toward trains and waiting for them—in fact, waiting for anything. The only other person in the station compound is a woman knitting. This can suggest imminent birth (the only other reference to knitting in the oeuvres describes a pregnant woman); in any event, her positive act contrasts with the poet's feelings of emptiness and frustration. Then he notices how "Shriveled moth eggs that had never hatched / stick to the huge clockface labelled Out of Order." Natural and unnatural orders of time both have failed, just as the poet has failed to catch his train.

Four elements characterize the traditional side of Kinoshita's aesthetic: the way he deals with nature, the immanence of poetry he finds in all things, faith in concrete imagery, and a paucity of themes. First we must note the characteristic manner in which he deals with nature in the broad sense.

Whenever the pressures of routinized existence threaten peace of mind, a traditional remedy in Japanese culture has been "return" to nature. While not unfamiliar to Westerners, such retreat has never been in Japan quite the romantic escape it often is in the West. During the 1930's and 1940's, in fact, the Japanese government extolled the fundamental values of the soil, urging the idea that farms comprised the basis of the nation (nōhonshugi). Official policy assumed that subordination to nature was supportive and cathartic, that nature teaches a man where his roots lie and shows him how to see himself more clearly, and that the "natural realm" cleanses and restores the psyche. Retreat to the countryside returns a person to an even keel, allowing him to continue as an effective and contributing member of society. Kinoshita, too, despite feeling as alienated as any modern urban intellectual, found that absorption in nature helped attenuate his bitterness and make life bearable. At least temporarily.

Tree poems exemplify the positive benefits of this relationship. Although not always as obvious as in "Treelike," the title poem of this collection, the collapse of distance between poet and tree allows the latter to blot up the poet's fears, anger, loneliness, and sense of being superfluous or estranged. That is why, after describing in this work how he resembles—or would like to resemble—a tree, Kinoshita concludes the poem from the perspective of enlightenment. He even imitates Buddhist rhetoric as he writes, "Because I have no-thing I have every-thing / because I am one I am all." This relationship with trees reflects the ancient Japanese belief that man never stands as an adversary to nature and that natural objects represent ideal forms of human existence. Like the lilies of the field that "toil not neither do they reap," trees for this poet represent "beings" that transcend life's emotional turmoil and embody the hope of equilibrium in the face of disaster, even death.

The second element of his aesthetic is partly a function of the first: Kinoshita believed that poetry lies immanent in all of creation. Because the whole earth inhabited him, as it were, daily life wherever he experienced it could provide valid material for poetry; every single phenomenon potentially stood as a correlative of what he was and what he felt. "Resin oozing like poems / from the cut ends of stacked logs" served as effectively as "lumps of coal in storage bins" to express him and inspire poetry. Poetic inspiration, in fact, imitates the possibilities of enlightenment: forever present in each person but not always experienced. Thus for Kinoshita no contradiction could exist between the way he sought his essential self and the truths of human existence under the leaves and in the grasses at Miyuki "as though searching for a violet," and the way an urban poet might seek them under the soot and in the cabarets of Tokyo.

Third, Kinoshita believed in the power of crisp imagery to communicate experience. Like countless poets before him, he left abstract ideas to thinkers or philosophers and concerned himself with the tangible and the phenomenal as he endeavored to deal with experience, its pains and its griefs. He interested himself less in whether the figure originated in the city or in the country than in whether it effectively opened a window to his feelings. For he apparently believed that the strength of an image derived from its dimensional solidity. If sufficiently substantial, an image will resonate with experience and thereby affect any reader who takes the trouble to re-create the scene in his mind. The imagination for Kinoshita throbbed with latent power; it could readily elicit any feeling or any insight so long as the poet expressed it through concretely visual language.

Any who read much of Kinoshita's work soon discover the fourth element, a paucity of themes. He tends to explore from many subtle angles a mere handful of ideas that reflect his strongest feelings. This occurs in part because of a perfectionistic drive to express himself to satisfaction and in part because of the indigenous concern to concentrate on moments of feeling or sentiment. The Japanese artist seems to believe, "I feel therefore I am." Consequently, writers like Kinoshita move ever inward in an attempt to capture some moment of awareness, less concerned to expand than to exploit their themes. They do not honor variation for its own sake, nor do they believe that each event or phenomenon is wholly disparate and entirely unique. Rather, these writers see all of reality in each and every solitary experience or aspect of nature. Reality lies deep within—in the kokoro, the heart of man, that which makes him truly human. So poets like Kinoshita prefer to focus on the inner realm of emotion, far more limited in scope than the realm of ideas.

*

Kinoshita's place in modern Japanese literature has not yet been firmly established. True, his first collection shared the prestigious Bungei Hanron Poetry Prize in 1940 and his posthumous collection won the Yomiuri Literature Prize for poetry and haiku in 1966. And a recent collection that includes thirty-four notable poets active since 1926 but presently deceased includes samples of his work. Yet critics tend to dismiss him as a traditional poet, and hence somewhat passé, rather than evaluate his artistic growth after 1955.

Based on what he has published since that time, Kinoshita certainly deserves reevaluation. Apart from his competence as a poet, apart even from the ability of his work to move people or give them pleasure, he stands as an important example of the links a poet can forge between his poetic past and contemporary experiments in free verse. He labored for years to wed rural and traditional sensitivities to the modern urban consciousness of estrangement and anxiety, never dealing with his heritage by repudiating it. That alone recommends more serious attention than has to date been given Kinoshita's poetry.

Kinoshita's total output of free verse was relatively small. Including his unpublished late-teen notebook containing eighty-four verses, he probably wrote fewer than 400 poems. This does not include nearly 600 haiku, dozens of lyrics he was asked to write for school or company songs, nor an unknown number of pieces solicited by area schools, magazines, and newspapers. I have selected at least one work from each of his eight books; this includes twenty from his first two collections, six prose poems, four verses written for children, and some two dozen from his last and most important collection, FLUTE PLAYER (1958); Appendix II includes three works from his teen-age notebook plus "The Wharf," a poem published before he graduated from middle school.

With seven exceptions, the poems have been translated from texts in TEIHON KINOSHITA YŪJI SHISHŪ (Collected Poetry of Kinoshita Yūji, 1966) and GANSHU NO SHIJIN: KINOSHITA YŪJI (Diffident Poet: Kinoshita Yūji, 1975), published on the tenth anniversary of the poet's death. Aside from the four works in Appendix II, "Exacta Ticket" was found among Kinoshita's effects after his death; his late brother kindly gave me the original hand written manuscript. "Horizontal Bar" appeared in a 1955 mimeographed collection of poems for children, and "Late Night Whistler" was published in the PHP magazine in 1960. The poems appear in chronological order; the date of each is given in Appendix IV: Index of Titles. Names follow the indigenous custom of placing the family name first.

Robert Epp

University of California
Los Angeles, 1982

ACKNOWLEDGEMENTS

Ibuse Masuji first urged me to translate his friend's poetry many years ago; I appreciate his warm encouragement. Kinoshita's widow, Miyako, and his late older brother, Takuji, kindly provided all information requested, copies of poems and documents nowhere else available, and endless hospitality on my visits to Miyuki. Professors Ben Befu, Iida Gakuji, and Ōhara Miyao answered countless questions about the meaning of the poems and, furthermore, laboriously compared earlier drafts against the original; Professor Nishihara Shigeru and Mrs. Kurita Motoye shared reminiscences and insights into the poet and his work. For comments on earlier drafts of the poems and/or the introduction, I thank Professors Arthur Kimball and Thomas Fitzsimmons, and Dr. Elva Kremenliev and Dr. Donald Brannan; they deserve credit for any graceful lines or clear logic. Finally, I am grateful to the Japan-United States Friendship Commission for financial support to publish these translations, which shared the first Friendship Fund Prize for literary translation.

Earlier versions of thirteen of these poems have appeared in CHELSEA ("Late Summer"), CONTEMPORARY LITERATURE IN TRANSLATION ("At the Temple," "Evening Scenes," "One Day of a Journey," and "The Pheasant"), LITERATURE EAST AND WEST ("A Lad," At an Inn," "Country Table," "Hinomisaki Village," and "Youthful Days" [1946]), and TRI-QUARTERLY ("At a Train Station," "February," and "Treelike"). The editors have kindly allowed me to reprint these poems in this collection.

TREELIKE

私は石炭のよう
に黒く黙っていたい
石炭のように、はげ
しく燃えたい

木下夕爾

I WANT

1963

POEMS/1939-1949

都会のデッサン

I

日曜日―僕らは幸福をポケットに入れてあるく　時どき取出したり

又ひっこめたりしながら　磨かれた靴　軽い帽子　僕らは独身もの

のサラリイマンです　さうして都会よ　君はいつでも新刊書だ　オ

レンヂエヱドの風のあとに　見たまへあの舗道の上　またもやプラ

タヌの並木の影はいつせいに美しい詩を印刷する　爽やかな拍手と

ともに

II

百貨店―エレベェタアよ　気が向いたら地獄まで墜ちてくれたまへ

天国まで昇ってくれたまへ―ここは屋上庭園だ　遠い山脈　そして

青空とアドバルゥン　ああ今僕らは感じる　あの金網の動物たちよ

りももっと悲しく　都会よ　君の巨きな掌(てのひら)に囚(とら)へられてゐる僕ら自

身を

PORTRAIT OF THE CITY

1.

Sunday—we stroll about with joy in our pockets now and then reaching for it or returning it   Polished shoes   summer hats   we white-collar bachelors   Oh city!   always a newly published book   In the wake of the orangeade wind look!   on the pavement   plane trees along the boulevard throw out shadows   print up lovely poems   to brisk applause.

2.

Department store—elevator!   drop us to hell or raise us to heaven   as you wish—the roof garden   the distant range   the blue sky   an ad-balloon   Ah now we feel more pathetic than caged animals   City! captive in your huge palm.

或る午後の手紙

今日　空はなんと明るいことだらう　街をあるきながら　ふと僕は
無花果の木にのぼりそこねたやうな人生嫌悪を覚えました　そんな
とき　百貨店へはいつていつて小便すると　まつしろいタイルの上
をながれるその美しい色が　多少とも僕を安心させ元気づけるので
す

――今日もまた若いプラタヌの並木の下には水のやうなメランコリ
イがあふれ　なんのおかまひもなしに空はじつに明るい　そして僕
は　とあるレストランにはいつてゆき　ひとりで　マカロニといつ
しよに　そんなに細長い自分の悲哀をたべるのです

AFTERNOON LETTER

Today   how bright the sky   Walking through town
I find myself loathing life as when I failed to shinny up our fig
tree   I go to the department store then and urinate
That beautiful color flowing over the snow white tiles   calms
and cheers me

Today a liquid mélancholie bubbles up again   under
that avenue of young plane trees   the sky so effortlessly
brilliant   I go to a restaurant   alone   and consume
with the macaroni   my so slender private griefs.

新しい季節の手

化学教室の白い窓框に
のびあがり　のびあがり
攀縁植物が優しい手をかける

その翼をヂュラルミンのやうに光らせて

友よ　また秋がやつて来た

ミクロスコオプのつめたい手ざはり
Organische Chemie のとある頁には
ひからびた蚊の死骸―僕たちのスウヴニイル
ときどき微風が来てのぞくので
上皿天秤は不安定だ
僕らの心のやうに

陽なたの石の上にゐる
死におくれた蠅の羽音を聴きたまへ
あるときは明るい幻聴のやうな
またあるときは悲哀の微粒子が
永遠のブラウン運動をしてゐるやうな……

賢い友よ　ここの草の上に来てすはれ
君の頭よりももっと早く
あの柘榴が熟れて来た

長い化学方程式のやうに
今日　僕ののどにひつかかるものはなんだらう
ああ草の上に臥てゐると
モズのこゑが僕らにするどいメスを入れる
そして何かをひっぱりだしては持つてゆく……

THE FINGERS OF A NEW SEASON

Reaching up   up
the vine touches gentle fingers to a white windowframe
in our chemistry classroom

Autumn has come along again my friend

wings glistening like duralumin

The cold touch of a microscope
the shriveled carcass of a mosquito (our trophy)
on a page of Organische Chemie
soft breezes sneaking in now and then
to unsettle the balance
as they unsettle my mind

Listen to fall's last fly buzzing
on a sunny rock
now a brightness imagined in the ear
now the endless Brownian movement
of pathetic particles . . .

Come sit on the grass here shrewd friend
That pomegranate has ripened
far faster than your brain

What catches in my throat today
like stringy chemical formulas?
When I stretch out on the grass
a shrike's cry jabs a sharp blade into me
plucks something out   carries it off . . .

早春の歌

1

わづかなメランコリイを
僕はギタアの穴のなかに押込んだ
とある郊外の
パラシュウトのやうにひらいた空の下で
僕はマンドリンに似た坂をのぼってゆく
僕の靴はよく乾いた雪を踏む
自分の悔恨ほどの雪を

2

春はもう遠く
世界のすみずみまであるきははつて

3

来る日も来る日もいい天気だ
猫柳は白く　娘の柔毛のやうに光る
僕のそばを
雲の影が大股に通りすぎる
桑畑で　頬白が音譜を書く
その尻つぽで　早春の音譜を

或る日の僕らの願ひのやうに
ああ陽に向いて立てる樹木たち
僕はそれをくぐつてゆく
春の門をくぐるやうに

SONGS OF EARLY SPRING

1.

Under a suburban sky
spread out like a parachute
I stuff some scraps of mélancholie
into my guitar
and labor up a mandolin shaped hill
crunching through snow
brittle as my remorse.

2.

Spring has already hiked
to the most distant corners of the world
Fine weather   day after day
pussy willows glistening bright as down on a maiden's arm
clouds walking beside me
with huge shadowy strides
a bunting in a mulberry orchard writing tunes
with its tail   tunes of early spring.

3.

Imitating onetime hopes
trees stand square into the sun
I duck under them
the way one passes through the gate to spring

そして丈の高い草を分けながら
菫を探すやうに
僕は探してゐる　もう一人の自分を

4

硫酸銅いろの湖には
小鳥の死骸や
破かれた楽譜が泛んでゐる
誰かの欝積した冬の弾丸が
たぶん君らを打貫いたのだらう
あ　啼きながら小鳥が来て水を浴びる
水を浴びる
いくつも小さい虹をつみかさねて……

and laying back the tall grass
as though searching for a violet
I search for that other me.

4.

Floating on the lake's copper sulphate glow
a bird's carcass
a tattered musical score:
bullets from someone's pent-up winter
probably ripped them through
Look!   chirruping   a bird comes to bathe
and splashes up rainbow
after tiny rainbow.

スコオル

ながい晴天のあとに
アンブルグラスのやうに光る一隊が来て
この村を洗つた
僕のパンセを洗つた
あらゆる乾いてゐるものを洗つた
そして美しい陽の下で
ブロンズの立像にこびりついた小鳥の糞が
新しい薬品のやうに光り出す
新しい薬品のやうに

SQUALL

After a long stretch of clear skies
a band of clouds sparkling like ampules
visited our hamlet
rinsed my pensée
rinsed every dried-out thing
and under this lovely sun
bird droppings crusted on the bronze statue
glisten like fresh medicine
like fresh medicine.

村

Fragments

村はあらひたての浴衣のやうだ
薄荷いろの　上等でないサボンの匂ひがする
それはこわばつてゐて　そして寂しい
けれど麦笛の音はじつによくひびく
僕たちは麦笛をならしに行かう

＊

藪のほとりに澄んだ眼をした
山羊がすはつてゐる
僕のやうに
彼のヒゲほどの雨が
水の上でふるへる

＊

無花果の木のかげに牡牛が眠つてゐる
僕のまねをして
退屈（アンニュイ）のやうに　おほきな曲りくねつた角を
彼はもてあます

おお僕もここで年老いるでせう
明るい螺旋のほとりで永遠に虹が歌ふやうに

＊

最後の夕映だ
地球は明るい　そして
僕らの村もあかるい
野菜畑にゐる家畜の眼はうるんで
少年のやうだ
僕らは河の方へ出よう
オフェリヤの頬のやうな水のひかりを眺めよう

VILLAGE*

Fragments

My village a freshly laundered yukata
the aroma of cheap mint colored soap
still and cheerless
But barley straws make such nice whistles
let's make the straw sing!

*

A clear eyed goat
rests at thicket's edge
like me
rain sparse as his beard
quivering on the water.

*

A bull dozes under a fig tree
imitating me
like ennui his huge twisted horns
too much for him
Yes I suppose I too shall age here
a horsefly buzzing forever near a shiny coil.

*

Sunset's final flush
The earth cheerful
our village cheerful too
The eyes of livestock in the vegetable garden
blurry as the eyes of young boys
Let's go to the river and watch the water glow
like Ophelia's cheeks.

15

田舎の食卓

乾草いろの歳月が燃される
僕のまはりで
あの蜜蜂の翅の音が
僕を煮る
悲哀の壺で
ああ　とろ火で

COUNTRY TABLE

Time the hue of hay
burns everywhere around me
the buzz of honeybees
stewing me
in a crock of griefs
yes   over a flame that simmers.

少年

毒蛇の舌のやうにやはらかい雨が
南の方から来て頬を濡らした
僕はいつも美しい包装の本を持つてあるいた
自分の秘密のやうに
誰もゐないところでそれをひらいて見るのだつた
五月のくさむらにねころぶと
いきなり大きい腕が僕を目隠しするのだつた……

A LAD

Soft as a snake's tongue
rain from the south licks my cheeks
I always carry a book with pretty wrappers
to open when I am quite alone
like a private secret
As I stretch out on a patch of May grass
huge hands suddenly cover my eyes . . .

秋のほとり

Fragments

厚ぼつたい本を閉ぢるやうに夏が終つた
宿題を終へた中学生のやうに
僕らはもう思ひ出さないだらう
地の果に消えた
幾何学的な線をもつた雲の連なりを……
僕らの手にあるのは
乾からびた美しい昆虫の死骸ばかりだ
防腐剤の匂ふ新しい木の箱に
僕らはピンでそれを留める
僕らのスウヴニイルといつしよに

  *

僕は空気のつまつた銃を肩にする
僕は犬を連れる
犬は犬の尻つぽの先にゐる
林のなかには光線がぎつちりつまつてゐる
けれどどの樹にもポケットがないので寂しさうだ
枝枝を透かして空は青いリトマス紙のやうだ

縞のシャツを著た若い男が樹を伐つてゐる
ふと僕は空想する
あの切口から新しい光線がほとばしつて
逆にあの男を伐り倒しはしないかと……

  *

青い封筒に入れて蔵ひわすれた
サルフィヤの種子が気にかかるやうに
友よ 今日僕は君の消息が気にかかる
空が美しい絞首台をひろげてゐる
のこりすくない玉蜀黍の髪を風がゆさぶつてゐる
金木犀がぷんぷん匂つてゐる

AUTUMN'S EDGE*
Fragments

Summer ended the way one shuts a ponderous tome
Like the high-school student who just finished his homework
we probably do not recall
the rows of clouds whose geometrical tracks
disappeared beyond the horizon . . .
all that's left of summer:
the shriveled carcasses of beautiful insects
pinned to new wooden boxes
that reek of preservative
like our other souvenirs.
*
A cocked airgun on my shoulder
I lead my dog
my dog leads his tail
Lightbeams jampack the grove
but trees grieve not having pockets
sky among the branches   a blue litmus
A young man in a striped shirt cuts down a tree
and I find myself imagining
that a fresh lightray freed by the wounds
might turn the tables and fell him . . .
*
Your news today upsets me my friend
the way those salvia seeds filed and forgotten
in a blue envelope distress me
Sky sets up a lovely gallows
wind teases the last few tassles of corn
a daphne fills the air with fragrance

さうして　小さい坂や
黒い板塀がつづいてゐることまで
ああみんな今日はおあつらへむきだ
せきこんで
君が　君の好きなチェホフの話をするには

*

啼いてゐる小鳥の胸のやうに
磧は白く光ってゐる
僕の空想のごとく曲りくねった河岸に沿うて
マリゴォルドの花が咲く
友よ
僕の生活は相も変らず
タデ科の植物の実のやうに乏しいが
しかし僕はノンキでないことはない
（それが老人のものであるのをいとはないなら！）
たまたま草の上にぼんやりしてゐると
アヒルの群が僕を急きたてる

even a gentle slope
and a stretch of black clapboard fence
Everything perfect now
for you to rattle on impetuously
about your beloved Chekov.
*
The dry gully glistens white
like the breast of a chirping song bird
marigolds bloom
along a riverbank sinuous as my visions
Though my livelihood
remains as sparse
as smartweed seeds
I can be carefree my friend
(if you don't mind a carefree dotard)
When I stand dreamily on the grass
a flock of ducks comes by to goad me on.

街上某日

1

よごれた紙幣を手にして
暗い石づくりの銀行を出たとき
ぱらぱらと霰が肩をたたいた
うしろから　ふるさとの顔なじみがはなしかけるやうに
あわただしい街のざわめき

僕はゆれる隠花植物のひとむれを見る
僕は眠つてゐる家畜を見る
僕は晴れた日のパセリ畠の匂ひを嗅ぐ

2

あかるい陽がまた地上にもどつてきた
つかのま過ぎた祭よ　舗道の上で息絶える　寂しい祭よ

僕は故郷への手紙を書いた　切手のみどりが眼にしみた

とあるレストランで僕はコオヒイをのんだ
土いろのコオヒイを
それから　エレベエタアで百貨店の屋上に出た

遠くに　あざやかに晴れわたる山脈の貌を見た

ONE DAY IN THE CITY

1.

When I left the Bank's stony gloom
dirty bills in hand
hail beat on my shoulders
The busy street's bustle sounded like
a hometown friend calling from behind

I see a clump of swaying ferns
and dozing cattle
I smell a parsley patch on a clear day.

2.

Bright sun comes back to the earth
Fleeting holiday! Choking on the pavement my lonely holiday!
I write a letter home   the green of the stamp stings my eyes
I have some coffee at a restaurant
dirt colored coffee
then take an elevator to the roof of the department store
I gaze at the crisp clear ranges in the distance.

旅舍

僕はよごれた襯衣を脱ぐ
きたならしい若さを脱ぐやうに
僕はあたらしい襯衣を著る
晴れた日の蓬の匂ひを嗅ぎながら

夜が母親のやうな雨をつれて来た
それはいつまでも窓の下に佇んでゐる
灯を消して僕がねむるのを見とどけるまで

AT AN INN*

I slipped off my dirty undershirt
the way I slipped out of my sordid youth
and put on a clean shirt
savoring the scent of yomogi on this clear day

Night brought motherly rains
They'll loiter beneath my window
to check that I blow out my lamp and sleep.

ゆふぐれ

1

小さい風が来て教会の木をゆする
その葉うらにまだのこつてゐた
うたごゑとおるがんの音がゆれる
枝枝の間に青空はつめたく澄んで
祈祷するひとびとの瞳のやうだ

2

蜘蛛の巣はその手でとらへてゐる
今さつきとほつていつた驟雨と
とほい夕映と
基督のやうにやせた
昆虫の死骸とを

EVENING

1.

Gentle winds rock those trees by the church
Lingering beneath their leaves
the trembling of choir voices and organ melodies
The branch-framed skies look coolly luminous
like eyes at prayer.

2.

The fingers of the spiderweb have caught
the squall that just passed by
sunset's distant glow
the carcass of an insect
gaunt as Christ.

帰来

僕はゐる　さまざまの場所に
昔のままのやさしい手に
責められたり　抱かれたりしながら

僕はそこにもゐる
酸つぱいスカンポの茎のなかに
それを折るときのうつろな音のなかに

僕はそこにもゐる
トカゲみたいに臆病さうに
陽のあたる石の上に
柿若葉の下かげに

僕はそこにもゐる

ながれのほとりの草の上に
とらへそこねた幸福のやうに
魚の光る水のなかに

僕はそこにもゐる
土蔵のかげ　桑の葉のかげに
アイヌ人みたいに
口のほとりに桑の実の汁の刺青をして

僕はそこにもゐる
小鳥が巣を編む樹の梢に
屋根の上に
略奪の眼を光らせて

僕はそこにもゐる

GOING HOME*

I'll be in many places
rejected or embraced
by arms as tender now as they ever were

I'll be
in a sour sorrel stem
in the hollow sound it makes when snapped in two

I'll be
under young persimmon leaves
on a sun drenched rock
timid as a lizard

I'll be
on grass along the stream
in water glistening with fish
like joys that slithered from my grasp

I'll be
by the storehouse under our mulberry tree
tattooing my mouth with mulberry juice
like an Ainu

I'll be
on treetops where songbirds build their nests
on rooftops
eyes glaring with plunder

I'll be

しその葉のいろのたそがれのなかに
とほくから草笛のきこえる道ばたに
人なつかしくネルの着物きて

ああ僕はそこにもゐる
井戸ばたのほのぐらいユスラウメの木の下に
人を憎んで
ナイフなんど砥いだりしながら

fondly wearing my flannel kimono
of an evening mauve as a shiso leaf
listening by the roadside to reed flutes in the distance

Ah   I'll be
under those shadowy ruby plums by the well
loathing that friend
honing my knife.

田舎の理髪店で

幼馴染の体は石鹸の匂ひがぷんぷんする
石鹸の匂ひのやうに　このわかい男にも
もう生活が染みこんでゐるのであらう

鏡に映つてゆれる
木橋と濁つた水と
彼の顔と──(頤のところの小さい疵はあの時の喧嘩のあとだ)

金がなくなつて　またかへつて来た男の悲しみを
彼は器用に剃りあげる
昨日　川から腐つてあがつた水死人の話をしながら

ああ僕の瞳のうらで
昔のままの木橋がゆれる
濁つた水が流れる──二十年の歳月が……寂しい怒りのやうに

AT A COUNTRY BARBERSHOP

My boyhood friend reeks of soap
Though young his livelihood already saturates him
like the scent of soap

They flicker across the mirror
that wooden bridge   the muddy waters
his face (the small chin scar from a childhood fight)

Talking of the bloated corpse on the river yesterday
he deftly shaves away the griefs of this fellow
who ran out of money and came back home

In my mind's eye
the bridge quivers as it did long ago
muddy waters flowing—
twenty years . . . like lonely rage.

L'ESPOIR

コルベンのかたちをして、
畠のなかで太つてくる
百合科植物の球根よ
私の思想もそのやうに
どつしりとしてありたいものだ
昨日ブナの古木からとつてきた
つきよ茸よ
私の半生も
おまへのやうな光をもちたいものだ
暗い厨のかたすみでも——

L'ESPOIR

Flask-shaped
lily bulb
fattening in the field!
I wish my thinking
had your weight
Moon mushroom
brought in yesterday from an old beech log!
I wish my half life ahead
might glow like you
if only in gloomy kitchen corners . . .

生れた家

眼にちかい海　一つの波が牆をとびこえる
とびこえてすぐに息絶える　若い波がまた立ちあがる
麦藁帽子のやうにゆれる日まはり
白い水着についた松の花粉
わらひごゑ　光る汗のアスピリン
私は古い椅子の上にゐる　私のうしろに家がある
家は大きい　さうして私のなかでは傾いてゐる
厨で魚を焼く匂ひ　食器をあらふ音
かつて私のすてたものがいま私をとりかこむ
牕から母親がよびかける　若若しい声で
黄いろい書物が私の手からすべりおちる
よはよはしい憤怒のやうに　風がしきりに頁をめくる
私のために　母親のために　そのほかの人のために──

THE HOUSE WHERE I WAS BORN

Sea crowds my eyes   a wave clears the wall
and clearing spends itself as others build
Swaying sunflowers imitate straw hats
flecks of pine pollen dot white bathing suits
laughing voices   shining aspirins of sweat . . .
I sit on an old chair in front of the house
sinking hugely within me
Smells of broiled fish and sounds of tableware
things I once rejected now besiege me
Mother's sprightly voice calls from the kitchen window
a yellowed book slips from my hands
As though in anemic rage wind rapidly flips its pages
for me   for Mother   for all . . .

昔の歌　Fragments

夜が来た　夜よ　壮麗な夏の昼が夜のなかに蔵はれる　さうして私
も蔵ひこまれるのだつた　見しらぬ大きいもののなかに――

　　――毎夜　私はリルケの詩集を枕がみにおいてねむつた　小さな灯
の下で　その白い頁のところどころに　草の汁でついた指紋がうね
つてゐた　それゆゑ私は　いつでも晴れた日のくさむらにすわるこ
とができた　さうして　私は捕へることができた　幸福を――帽子
を投げて昆虫を捕へるやうに

明けがたの林のなかのプロムナアドよ――しかし私がそこを通るの
は　いつも神神の祝祭のをはつたあとだ　空に向つて背のたかい椅
子の足がならび　パン屑みたいな花が点点とこぼれている……　樹
脂が固まつてゐる　寂しいパンセのやうに　ときをり　池がジレッ
トのやうに光つて　まだ私の額につかまつてゐる夢をそぎ落す……

SONGS OF OLD

fragments

Night has come   Night!   A magnificent summer day
shrouded in night   and I shrouded in it too   in something
huge   something unfamiliar . . .

—Night after night   I went to bed with a book of Rilke's poems by
my pillow   Under my dim lamp   I saw where grass-stained
fingers had meandered from place to place   over the book's
white pages   That's how I could always sit in the grass on sunny
days   and catch   happiness—like catching some bug with a
cast of my cap

My promenade through the grove at daybreak!—But I passed
through   only after the gods had finished their festivals
Rows of tall chairs   their backs reaching for sky   flowers
scattered here and there like breadcrumbs   resin hardening
like lonely thoughts . . . Even now the pond   sparkles like a
Gillette blade   to slice away those dreams still stacked on my
forehead . . .

私は好んだ　青空と木の梢がつくり出す　あのエエテルのやうな世
界を　また　風と水とがゆがく　あの美しい甃の世界を――ときを
り私はそこに在りたいと希つた――けれどももしそれが出来たら
ああ　母上よ　たぶん私はすぐにかへつて来るでせう　かへつて来
て　小さい刃ものの傷でいつぱいな机の前にすわるでせう　さうし
て母上よ　私は　あの花の種子を蒔いたかどうかをたづねるでせう
ゐなくなつた犬のことを話したりするでせう

I loved the ether-like world   made with bluesky and treetops
and I loved that beautifully pleated world—painted with wind and
water—sometimes I've wished I were there—But if I could be
ah   Mother!   I would most likely come straight home instead
       Once home   I might sit at that desk with all those penknife
nicks   And Mother!   I might ask whether you had planted
your flower seeds   and we'd talk about things like the dog we
once had.

伐材

斧の音がきこえる　斧の音の木魂がきこえる　きれいにつみかさね
られた空気の層がふるへて　樹木のなげきの身ぶりをつたへる　な
らべられた彼らの腕の切口に　樹脂が滲み出る　涙のやうに　木洩
れ陽に光りながら……

　　　　＊

ふかく打ちこんだ斧は　しばらくは抜けない　樹木はしつかりと斧
をつかまへるのだ　あらはなその肌の傷口をかくさうとするやうに

　　　　＊

夏の日の午後
私はその樹の蔭でねむつた
本を読んだり　馬鹿らしい空想にふけつたりした
今日　ざはめく水のやうに
私は浴びる　伐り倒される樹木たちの影を
斧よ　鳴れ
さうしてはやく伐り倒せ　その樹を
退屈で長かつたわが夏の日も

LOGGING

I hear an axe echoing   Beautifully sandwiched air layers quiver
and report the tree's gestures of grief   Resin oozing from wounds
in its ranked arms glisten like tears   in sunlight shifting through
branches . . .

*

        The deeply biting axe wedges momentarily
The tree trunk grips it firmly as though to cover naked
scars.

*

One summer afternoon
I dozed in the shade of that tree
reading a book and indulging foolish reveries
Like rustling waters
I bathe today in the shade of trees awaiting the axe
Let it echo loudly
as it quickly fells these trees   and with them
my long my listless summer day.

旅の一日

気楽な捕虜になるために僕の心はすぐに碇をおろしたがる

もうこの碇を引揚げよう　僕はトランクのなかにシャツやなんか

をおしこむ　僕は書物をおしこむ　僕は僕をおしこむ

さあ出発だ　さようなら　僕は挨拶する　誰もゐないのに

風が僕の靴をみがく　きれいな流れのほとりで　娘が髪をあらつ

てゐる

藪のそばに牛と羊がねむつてゐる　さようなら　僕はかへるんだ

よ　僕は帽子をとる　誰もゐないのに　木犀の匂ひが　長いこと僕

を追つかける　まもなく僕は小さい停車場に出るだらう　赤い舌の

やうな切符に　としよりの駅員がゆつくり鋏を入れる　僕の悲しみ

ほどの穴をあける　そして僕は古風な汽車に乗り　ああ二度とこん

なところを通らないだらう

ONE DAY OF A JOURNEY*

I feel tempted to drop anchor straightaway and make myself a carefree prisoner here

Let me weigh that anchor now   I stuff my shirts and things into a suitcase   I stuff my books   I stuff myself

Well   time to leave   I call Sayonara!   though no one's there

Wind polishes my shoes   a girl washes her hair beside a limpid brook

Cows and sheep drowse near the thicket   Sayonara! I'm going home   I tip my hat   though no one's there Daphne aromas persistently trail me   Soon I arrive at the tiny station An aged attendant leisurely punches my red tongue-like ticket making a hole the size of my sorrow   and I board the antique coach   Oh I'll not come here again.

或る秋の午後

就職試験をうけたかへりみち
僕は　とある脳病院のそばをとほった
その日の結果をあれこれと思ひめぐらしながら──
脳病院はひつそりして　ものおとひとつなかった
ふと僕は憶つた　発狂した友のことを
死ぬ日まで　やさしい恋歌をうたつたといふその男のことを
秋であつた
まつさをに空は晴れてゐた
手にしてゐた新刊書の包装ばかりが派手で美しく
靴のさきやシャツのよごれが　僕はひどく気になつた
人間の脳膸のやうに　柘榴が笑みわれてゐた
とつぜん　堪へがたい重さで
おそろしい真昼の寂しさが僕の肩を襲うてきた

AN AUTUMN AFTERNOON

Coming home from a job interview
weighing the day's harvest
I passed an asylum
silent   hushed
and remembered a friend gone mad
the one who sang sweet lovesongs till the day he died
It was autumn
the sky a deep clean blue
only the wrapping on my new book flashy and beautiful
my soiled shoes and shirt really bothered me
A burst pomegranate   picture of the brain . . .
suddenly I shouldered the intolerable weight
of a fearful midday emptiness.

訪墓記

傾きながら晩い夏の日が輝いてゐる
木の梢に　乾いた谷川の礫の上に

今私はやすんでゐる　帽子をとつて
杖のやうに影を傍らによこたへて

今私はやすんでゐる　蝶のやうに
おまへの憶ひ出の上にとまつて

手桶の水に小さな雲が映つてゐる
私はそれをおまへの顔だとおもふ

ああ蟬が鳴いてゐる　遠くで
鳴いてゐる　すぐ頭の上で

おまへのやうにはやく鳴きやんだ
蟬もゐるのだらう　あの中には

あのやさしいこゑが虚空に途絶え
やがて永く失はれる　人には知られずに

そして私もまた忘れてしまふのだらう
忘れるともなしに　激しい別な声にまぎれて

VISIT TO A GRAVE*

Late summer's setting sun glitters
on treetops on pebbles in the waterless ravine

I rest now taking off my hat
laying my shadow beside me like a cane

I rest   a butterfly
visiting reminiscence

Water in my bucket mirrors a cloud puff
I think of as your face

Ah cicadas sing in the distance
sing directly overhead

Among them one
who may stop singing as young as you

That tender voice suspended in space
then lost forever   unrecognized

I too may find myself forgetting   or perhaps only
beguiled by other more strident voices.

日の御崎村

松嶺をくぐりぬけると
いちめんの桑畠
その葉のかげにねむつてゐる漁村が見える

ここ出雲の国の突端の
空と水の何といふ明るさ

短い旅の日の午後に
激しい海鳴りに憑かれながら
私はふと死といふことを考へた
いつの日また私はこの代赭色の土を踏むだらう
あてもなく家を出て
はるかなものにあこがれたこの記憶はどこへ消え去るであらう

仰ぎみる六月の陽のもとに
燈台は長い影を曳いて立ち
黝ずんだ桑の実に無心な蟻が群れてゐた

HINOMISAKI VILLAGE*

Once I duck under the sighing pines
I see an expanse of mulberry trees
and beyond their leaves a sleepy town

How bright the air how bright the water
at this tip of Izumo

Haunted by the fierce pounding of waves
on the afternoon of my short day's journey
I find myself thinking of Death
When will I walk this ochre soil again?
Where will memories of thirst for the far off go
as I wander aimlessly from home?

Under the June sun high above
the lighthouse stands trailing its long shadow
and rapt ants throng the blue-black mulberries.

日の御崎村にて

その一

ここに来て
夏草の上
燈台の長き影踏む

ここに来て
わがひとり幼なごころに
丘の辺の桑の実を摘む

わがひとり
旅の日の暮るるも知らで

その二

ここに来て
何をか思ふ

ただ在るは
太古より絶ゆるとしなき
海鳴りと松吹く風と
かすかなるわがいのちのみ

風にとぶ草の絮より
なほ小さきわがいのちのみ

AT HINOMISAKI VILLAGE

1.

I come here
and pace on summer grass
the long lighthouse shadow

I come
alone   joyous as a child
and pick mulberries near the hill

Alone and quite unaware
that my day's journey will end.

2.

I come here
to think

Only sea roar and wind in the pines
ever since ancient times
only my frail life

only my life   slighter
than a dandelion seed in the wind.

若き日

晴れた日の丘の草を藉きながら一人が言つた
──もう百年もしたらきつといい時代が来るだらうと
他の一人がそれを笑つた
もう一人は黙つてゐた
三人とも若く悩むことが多かつた

その丘は今でもあそこにひろがつてゐる
昔と同じやうに老いた芒がなびいてゐる

遠い未来を信じたあの一人は早く死んだ

YOUTHFUL DAYS*

They sat under clear skies on a grassy hilltop
One said, "In a century good times will surely come"
That made another laugh
The third said nothing
All three youths had much to lament

That hilltop hasn't changed
frayed eulalia sways as in days long passed

He who trusted in the distant future died young

激しい思想の持主であつた他の一人はとらへられて獄に下つた

もう一人は家庭を持つて貧しく暮した

そして彼は秋晴れの丘をあるきながら

時をりあの言葉を思ひ出した

──もう百年もしたら……

無心にそよいでゐる羊歯の葉のさまが思ひ泛ぶのだった

the one with violent thoughts ended up in jail
the third had a family and lives in poverty
When he roams that hilltop under autumn's clear skies
he sometimes recalls the words
"In a century . . ."

Then for no reason
he sees visions of fern leaves
flickering aimlessly in sun's fluid light.

遠き都へ

あたらしきセルの着物のやさしさよ
母がなさけを身につけて
ふるさとの夜のやはらかさよ
花茨ほのかに白きそぞろあるきに
ああこの切なく肌に触るるもののゆゑに
わがこころまたあたらしく
遠き都へ去らんとす

TO THE FAR-OFF CAPITAL

The affection in my new serge kimono!
Wrapped in Mother's love
the comfort of an evening in my village . . .

What so poignantly warms me
as I walk by brambles blooming faintly white
lets me think again of going back
to the far-off capital.

旅のをはり

別れぎわに宿の娘が
庭に熟れた柚の実を一つ拵いでくれた

その実をてのひらに弄びながら
停車場までの道は長かった

やがて雪にうもれる
山脈の襞の深さよ

停車場の柵に凭れて
柚の実を弄びながら
私は長いこと上りの汽車を待ってゐた

JOURNEY'S END*

As I was saying goodbye
a girl from the inn gave me a ripe citron
she'd picked in the yard

I fondled the fruit
on the long way to the station

How deep the folds in those hills
soon to be buried in snow

I leaned against the fence at the station
and fondled my citron
waiting interminably for the inbound train.

哀春小曲

わたしは鎌です
そして刈られる穂麦です

明日といふ日がないやうに
あたしはきらめく知慧の鎌です
そして日ごとに刈られてゆく
哀しみの穂麦です

ARIETTA: SPRING GRIEFS

I the sickle
I the barley to be reaped

I the wise sickle that gleams
as though tomorrow might never come
I the grains of grief
reaped day after day.

晩　夏

停車場のプラットホームに
南瓜の蔓が匍いのぼる

閉ざされた花の扉のすきまから
てんとう虫が外を見ている

軽便車が来た
誰も乗らない
誰も下りない

柵のそばの黍の葉つぱに
若い切符きりがちよつと鋏を入れる

LATE SUMMER*

A squash tendril creeps up
to the platform of this small station

A ladybug peers from the folds
in one bud

The commuter train arrives
No one gets on
No one gets off

The young ticket taker nonchalantly punches
a millet leaf growing by the fence.

秋の日

ひとりでそそぐ湯のなかで
お茶がみどりの葉をのべるのがいい
長いあいだ蔵（かく）していて
遠慮ぶかくひろげる深いみどりがいい

AUTUMN DAY

Let tea leaves expand
in the hot water I pour on them
let the deep green so long held in
swell fully   with restraint.

夜学生

鞭の影が
地図の上に
のびたりちぢんだりする

先生の声がとぎれると
虫の音が部屋にみちてくる

学問のたのしさ
そしてまた何というさびしさ

本の上に来て
髭をふる
しべりあの地図より青いすいっちょよ

NIGHT SCHOOL STUDENT

The pointer's shadow
stretches and shrinks
across the wallmaps

At pauses in the teacher's talk
insect voices fill the room

The joys of study
and what sadness

Alighting on my text
a katydid greener than the map of Siberia
flourishes its feelers.

停車場にて

上りの汽車は出てしまった
がらんとした構内に
柚の実の匂いがのこっている
これも乗りおくれたらしい婦人がひとり
ベンチにもたれて編みものをはじめている
不正と貼り紙のしてある大時計のおもてに
孵らなかった蛾の卵がひからびている

AT A TRAIN STATION *

The inbound had just pulled out
The pungent odor of a citron tree hovers
in the abandoned station compound
A woman who also seems to have missed the train
rests on a bench and begins to knit
Shriveled moth eggs that never hatched
stick to the huge clockface labelled Out of Order.

東京行　　近江卓爾兄に示す

金をこさえて東京へ行つて来よう
そう思つて縄をなつている

行つてどうということもないが
昔住んでた大学町附近
過ぎ去つた青春について今さら悲歎にくれてもみたい思いがする
（われ等ははや未来よりも過去の方が多くなつた）
けれどどうにかまとまりかけると汽車賃が倍になる
縄ない機械を踏む速度ではとても物価に追いつけない
私のこの足はすでに東京の土を踏んでいるかも知れない
ないあげた縄の長さは北海道にも達するだろう

冬ざれの野原の見わたせる仕事場へ
わが子はふところ手でかえつてきて
けさは池に厚い氷が張つたという
霜に濡れたビナンカヅラの実を縁側にならべ
クリスマスのお菓子をこさえようという

TO TOKYO

for Ōmi Takuji

Hoping to make some money for a trip to Tokyo
I braid rope

Nothing special to do in Tokyo
I just think it's time to mourn my youth
lost in the university district where I lived long ago
(by now Takuji we have more past than future)
Yet whenever I get enough together the train fare doubles
I just can't work the braider fast enough to keep up with prices
I've treadled enough to be in Tokyo by now
I've braided enough rope to reach Hokkaido

Hands in pockets my child comes back to where I work
a room overlooking withered fields
She says there was a thick layer of ice on the pond this morning
Spreading her frosty red berries on the veranda
she tells me she'll make some Christmas candy.

昔 の 家

二三人の仲間といっしょに
僕はしばらくあの家に住んでいた
貧乏が誇りであった時代
悲しみがよろこびであった時代

今でも憶えている
南へひらく二階の窓
ゼラニウムのはちがひとつ
古びた油絵がかかっていた

今見知らぬ人人が住んで
明るい ともしびが道までこぼれ
楽の音とさざめきがながれてくる

あれもみな僕のものだ
僕のものであったのだ
僕たちがあの家へおいてきたのだ
つくづくとそう思う

THE OLD HOUSE

I lived awhile in that house
with two or three others
when poverty was pride
and misery joy

I still remember clearly
my second-floor window facing south
a lone pot of geraniums
a timeworn oil painting on the wall

People I've never seen live here now
bright light spills onto the street
music and voices fill my ears

They're mine
at least they once were mine
I'm absolutely sure I left them all
in this house.

POEMS/1950-1958

クリスマス・イヴ

あれは風の音です
虚空に消えたコーラス隊の合唱です
今や一つに集って
家々の戸をうちならす

空いっぱいにきらめく星は
凍りついたひとつひとつの鐘の音です
わたしの知らぬひとびとの
愛と祈りの涙です

おおクリスマス
わたしの神様

こころもこごえる寒さだけを
ことしも配りに参られた

CHRISTMAS EVE

Sounds of wind
chorusing voices that melt into space
join now to carol
in the entranceways of every home

Each star sparkling in the sky
a tinkle from a frozen bell
a teardrop of prayers and love
from people I do not know

Christmas!
My God

has given me again this year
only chills that ice the mind.

馬券

ついふらふらと馬券を買った
1と6の連勝式
当ったのは6と1
一六勝負の思いつきを
もうひとひねりすればよかった
おお　もうひとひねり
おれの詩も　このおれ自身も

EXACTA TICKET

In the end I bought it with qualms
for 1 and 6 to win and place
What paid was 6 and 1
If only I had made a slight switch
in my one/six hunch
oh just a slight switch
for my poetry   for me.

葉 桜

さしかわす枝の中の
ゆれさわぐ葉の中の
あの空だけがなぜ特別に美しいのだろう
さくらの樹は
あそこにまだ花の幻をもっているからだ
美しい仕事を終えたあとの
誇りとやすらいにみちているからだ

NEW LEAVES ON CHERRY TREES

Why is the sky so uncommonly beautiful
that floats among intermingled branches
among leaves trembling with excitement?
Because the cherry trees
retain visions of their blooming
because they teem with pride and repose
after finishing their lovely work.

冬の夜の歌

しづかな夜がきた
頬杖をついて
傷だらけの机によりか、るように
自分の孤独によりか、るときがきた
朝から鳴りやめなかった北風も
今はどこかへいなくなった
あの激しい怒りや悲しみにも
落ちつくことの出来る場所があるのだ
そう思うとふしぎにわが心もしづまるのだ

WINTER NIGHT

Still night has come
time to lean on loneliness
the way I lean chin in hand
on my nicked-up desktop
Even northwinds wailing steadily since dawn
have left now for places
where fierce rage and regrets as well
can find repose . . .
the thought strangely settles my mind.

寒　林

谺が返つて来る　銃声のように
冬木の枝がさしかわす　銃眼のように
はるかなるひとよ
そこから私を狙え！　撃て！
ただ一発で私は仆れるだろう
弾をふかくに抱きとめて
はるかなるひとよ
私はすぐに息絶えるだろう

WINTER GROVE

An echo resounds like a gunshot
barren branches merge like gunsights
You in the distance:
take aim from where you are   Shoot!
You in the distance:
a single shot will fell me
Stopping your round deep within
I'll breathe my last.

公園にて

テニスの音が
ゆるやかに
喪われた時と今の間を往き来している

読みさしの書物を閉じて
私は樹の間の空を仰いだ

朴の幹のうす蒼い肌に
ナイフであなたの名を彫った
忘れるために　憶い出さないために

この仮綴の書物のように
やがてわが生もまた閉じられるであろう
夏にこぼれ散った草の実ほどの記憶を
残して

春蟬が鳴いている
ブロンズの立像に小鳥の糞が白く
楔形文字のように光っている

AT THE PARK

Sounds from the tennis courts
shuttle leisurely
between a lost time and now

Closing my unread book
I gaze into the branch framed sky

I carve your name
on the pale bark of a magnolia
so I'll forget so I won't remember it

One day my life too will end up
like this paperback
leaving memories small as grass seeds
scattered through summer

Spring locusts hum
Bird droppings on the bronze statue
glitter white like cuneiform.

赤い月

女の鯖売りが来た
一ぴきもらつて蕗の葉にくるんだまま
しばらく縁側で世間話をした
鯖売りの女も私の父のことを記憶していた
父はよくこうして字の見えなくなる時刻まで
幼い私のために絵本を読んだ
点燈夫が街のガス燈をつけてあるく
古い西洋の物語であつた
永い日も暮れかけた
私の村ではいつも点燈夫のかわりに夕風が
見えない手で家々のあかりをつけてあるく
私は井戸端へ出てなまぐさい手を洗つた
見るかす熟れ麦の中から
鯖の眼よりも赤い大きな月があがつて来た

RED MOON

A woman selling mackerel came by
I took one and gossiped awhile on the veranda
holding the fish wrapped in a butterbur leaf
The mackerel vendor remembered Father
who often read from a picture book to little me
that old Western tale about the lamplighter
walking through town to put on the gaslamps
reading till times like this when pages dimmed
My long day faded to dusk
Not a lamplighter but evening breezes walk through my village
their invisible wands brightening up the houses
I went to the well and washed the fish smell from my hands
Over the vista of ripened wheat had risen a huge moon
redder than the mackerel's eyes.

踏切にて

ここを通らなければならない理由はなかったのだ
ちょつと遠廻りする気にさえなれば
ほかに幾つも道はあつたのだ
結局その方が早かつたのだ
それが今わかつたのだ
もつと早く気がつけばよかつたのだ
だから腹が立つたのだ
遮断機の腕木にとまつて
鎌をふり上げる
枯草いろのかまきりよ

AT A GRADE CROSSING

There's no reason to take this road
Had I felt like going a bit out of my way
a number of other paths would do
In the end that would have been quicker
So much is clear to me now
If only I'd realized it sooner
I might not be so upset
A mantis the hue of withered grass
perches on the horizontal crossing gate
brandishing its sickles.

都の友へ

おれがつくった米だから
その米でついた餅だから
すこしだけれど君に送る
おれの半歳をつめこんで
こうしてきつくしばつて送る
この縄も自分でなったのだ
いい正月を迎えてくれ
いいたよりをきかせてくれ
手のあかぎれに縄がさわるたびに
顔をしかめてるなどとは思つてもくれるな

TO A FRIEND IN THE CAPITAL*

I grew the rice myself
and pounded it into mochi
so I'm sending you a little
I tied the package tight
cramming this half a year into it
I also made the rope
Have a nice New Year
send me some interesting news
Don't think about how I wince
when rope touches my chapped hands.

遠い町

くるみの木の
葉かげにみえる
遠い町

そだをたばねに
ついて来て
いつもながめる

あの町
二度しかゆけない
おぼんとお正月と

石をひろって
なげてみる
ちからいっぱい
なげてみる

THE DISTANT TOWN

Under the leaves
of a walnut tree
the distant town

I stare at it
everytime I come to fetch
bunches of brushwood

I can go only twice a year
Obon   New Year's
That town!

I pick up a stone
and toss it
flinging it
with all my might.

野なかのいっぽんみち

おばさんは
自分のショールをずらして
わたくしの首を包んでくれた

とおい　さむい
野なかのいっぽんみち

どのわらづかも
より合って
生きもののように
あたため合っている

とおい　さむい
野なかのいっぽんみち

PATH THROUGH THE FIELDS

My aunt
pulled down one corner of her shawl
and wrapped it round my neck

That long chilly path
through the fields

Stacked sheaves
huddle together
warming each other
like living things

That long chilly path
through the fields.

鉄棒

はっと
とびついて
つかむ
鉄棒
いっしょうに
つかむ
あの山の
雪のてっぺん

HORIZONTAL BAR

Look!
I jump up
to grasp
the horizontal bar
and take in hand
the snowy summit
of that distant peak
as well.

春の鐘

子供らよ鐘を撞け
やわらかに鐘を撞け

ゆく春の日は真昼
竹やぶを透く桃畠

子供らよやわらかに
鐘を撞け

この鐘の中に眠れる音を
遠くとおく放ちやれよ
遠くとおくあそばせよ

子供らよ
鐘を撞け

ゆく春の日は真昼
青春の丘の起き伏し

SPRING BELL

Children! Toll the bell
toll it tenderly

at noon on this fleeting spring day
a peach grove peeking through the bamboo thicket

Children! Toll the bell
tenderly

and send the sounds sleeping in it
off into the distance
let them range far   far into the distance

Children!
Toll the bell

at noon on this fleeting spring day
hills pulsing in their prime.

秋の日

細君ににげられてから
彼はひとりで暮していた
自分の子供を脊負い
手に買物籠をぶら下げていた
籠から大根や人参の葉がのぞいていた
その底にラムボオやボオドレエルの文庫本がかくされていることを
誰も知らなかった
（彼を知るもののほかには）
彼はそれをいつも
目だたぬようにして人にひけらかした
できれば彼は赤ん坊を手にぶら下げ
詩の本のはいった買物籠を脊に負いたかったろう

彼はアパートの三階の
出窓のところに腰かけていた

AUTUMN DAY

He's been living alone
since his wife left him
He straps the baby to his back
and hangs a shopping basket on his arm
carrot tops and radish leaves exposed
Only his friends
know about the paperbacks
the Rimbaud and Baudelaire buried at the bottom
He always
displays his books inconspicuously
though if he could he'd hang the baby on an arm
and strap the poetry to his back

Sitting on the balcony
off his third-floor apartment

居眠りしているらしかった

腕に繃帯を巻いていた

（ゆうべも酔っぱらったにちがいない）

こわれかけた手すりにもたれて

彼は今にも落ちてきさうであった

三階の下はかたいアスファルトである

落ちたらひとたまりもないだろう

そうしたら彼も彼の詩も

（彼だけでなく僕も僕らの詩も）

むざんに楽々と寝ころぶことができるだろう

彼はぼんやりと顔をこちらにむけた

彼の眼に街路に立つ僕がうつったかどうか

ふいに赤ん坊の泣く声がきこえた

彼はゆっくり立ち上って

よろめきながら部屋の中へひっこんだ

he seemed to be dozing
one arm bandaged
(certainly he was drunk again last night)
as he leaned against the wobbly railing
on the verge of toppling down

Below his third-floor perch   bare asphalt
so he wouldn't survive
Then he and his poetry
not to mention yours and mine
could sprawl out comfortably without a qualm

He turned his head dreamily my way
I'm not sure he noticed me standing by the road
Suddenly the baby cried
Getting up turtlelike
he vanished unsteadily into his flat.

たえまなく光り

たえまなく光り
自分に注ぎかける者の為にのみ
水車は動く
たえまなく揺さぶり匂い
自分にささやきかける者の為にのみ
水車小屋の穀物は脱皮する
距てられた外部と内部
別々にあふれている光と匂い
ああ行為と心のつながりにも似た
その美しい調和と結実とを今
小屋の壁の破れから大きな眼のように
麦藁色の日の光がのぞきこむ

SPARKLING INCESSANTLY

Sparkling incessantly
the waterwheel turns only
for one ready to concentrate on himself . . .
ceaselessly agitated and brimming with fragrance
the mill hulls grain only
for one ready to inspire himself . . .
inside and outside separated
one abrim with light one with redolence
like links between mind and act
Straw-hued sunlight peers now like a giant eye
through cracks in the mill wall
at that lovely harmony that lovely yield.

早春

麦の芽の三四寸
ねこやなぎの影がのぞきこむ
蜷(にな)の道もまだ短かい

ゆっくりと水車を押している雪解の水は
遠い谷間から出てきたばかりだ
水車小屋の板戸のすきまから
薄暗い内部へ射しこんでいるひとすじのひかり
(僕の内部へむけられる眼のように)

たえまなく揺れうごき匂い立ち
すこしずつ皮をぬいでゆく穀物
(それは僕自身の心だ)

麦の芽は三四寸
やわらかな雲の影
風の中のかすかなヒバリ
やすみなく水車を押している雪解の水は
遠い谷間から出てきたばかりだ

EARLY SPRING

Barley shoots stand finger high
pussy willow shadows peering through them
even the trails of marsh snails   still short

Water from the thaw slowly urging the waterwheel
flows fresh from the distant gorge
Through a chink in the millshed door
a single lightbeam probes the interior
like that eye addressed to my innermost self

Grain ceaselessly quivers and glows with fragrance
little by little stripping off the hulls
a mirror of my mind

Finger-high barley shoots
Soft cloud shadows
The dim form of a skylark on the wind

Water from the thaw restlessly urging the waterwheel
flows fresh from the distant gorge.

夏の歌

誰もがながく保ちえないものを
ヘルマン・ヘッセが歌つた
（みずみずしい樹木のみどり
森の郭公
山のはにかかる満月）

けれどもそれらはついに失われることがない
葉脈のようにそれらは
深くしずみ待ち成熟する
光の鞭の中で

厳酷の夏よ
麦のように稲のように
私を刈り取るものは誰？
私を植え育てるものは誰？

太陽と閉じることのない大きな眼のために
絶えず白い雲たちを押しのけているものは？

SUMMER SONG

Herman Hesse wrote poems
about things no one can preserve
    the verdant green of young trees
    a cuckoo in the forest
    full moon on the hillside

But in the end we never lose them either
Like veins in a leaf
they burrow deep amid rods of light
waiting   aging

Stern summer!
Who will gather me in
who will plant and raise me
like barley   like rice?

Who ceaselessly brushes aside white clouds
for the sun and the huge eye that never sleeps?

子供の広場

ここは子供の広場です
いつもの野球の広場です
やわらかい冬の日が
空地いっぱいに照っている

穴だらけのネットが
臨海学校でみた干網のように
長い影を曳いている

ピッチャーのモーションの輪の中に
白いアパートが来て浮かぶ
青い山と給水塔と

（子供よ　子供よ　子供らも
誰かがこの世へ投げてきた

美しい新しいボールです
転んではずんで跳ねまわる）

郊外電車があらしのように
審判の声を吹き消して通る
審判をつとめる酒屋さんの
リヤカーに積んだ空瓶が
キラリキラリ光っている

見物人はちょうど今
選手の数と同じです
一人遠く離れているのは
紙芝居のおじさんで
自転車に片足かけたまま

PLAYGROUND

Here   the children's playground
a year-round baseball field
soft winter sunshine
warming the lot

Dragging long shadows
the tattered backstop looks like those drying nets
we once saw on a school campout at the beach

Green hills   the water tower
a white apartment house
float into the pitcher's windup

(Children! Children! Children—you too
are pretty new balls
someone has pitched into the world
rolling   bouncing   spinning!)

A commuter train passes like a storm
fouling the umpire's call
Empty bottles stacked on that bike trailer
belonging to the saké dealer who serves as ump
glisten brightly

There are as many spectators now
as players
The picture story man
one foot on his bike pedal
a distant onlooker

ここは野球の広場です
明るい楽しい広場です
ミットのかたちをした雲も
空からじっとみています

（子供よ　子供よ　子供らが
負けた試合の靴の中から
ザラザラこぼれる砂のような
この世の苦味を知るにはまだ間がある
子供よ　子供よ　子供らが
体じゅう草じらみをつけながら
ボールを探して歩くように
自分自身を探す日も）

This is the baseball field
a cheerfully pleasant playground
Even mitt-shaped clouds watch
intently from their skies

(Children! Children! Children—you
have time yet to learn that life's bitterness
is like the sand filling your shoes
when you lose the game
Children! Children! Children—you
have time till the day you search for your selves
the way you hunt for the ball
peppering your clothes with burrs!)

道

　林道が尽きた
　夕焼にむかつて
　物干台のように飛ぶ

THE TRAIL

Having vanished through the grove
the trail leaps like a drying rack
into sunset.

南風

傾く首
閉じられる眼
草にしたたる血
鶏は
拗られながら
絶えず
羽毛のかたちで飛び立つ

SOUTHWIND

Bent neck
closed eyes
blood trickling on the grass
the hen
being plucked
keeps flying up
with her plumage.

僕は

僕はすぐに蒸発する
ブンゼン燈のひとあぶりにも
僕はすぐに気散する
僕はもういないのだ
どろどろに煮えつまる
フラスコの中には
おお
灼けたフラスコを握りしめる
その
永遠に熱い手よ

I TURN TO VAPOR

Instantly I turn to vapor
with but one pass over a Bunsen burner
evaporated
no longer
in the furiously bubbling
flask
Oh
that ever hot hand
holding the heated glass!

笛を吹くひとよ

笛を吹くひとよ
あなたが僕の笛を吹くとき、
そのとき僕はここから出てゆきます
あなたがうっとりしているとき
僕はもうここにはいない
あなたの指の先から
あなたの唇がしめした歌ぐちから
僕は急いで出てゆきます
この美しい真昼の
花の咲いている方へ
水の流れている方へ
遠くへ
もっと遠くへ
僕は出てゆきます
笛を吹くひとよ

あなたが僕の笛を吹くとき
あなたがザインをゾルレンにかえるとき
そのとき僕はもうここにはいない
笛を吹くひとよ
笛を吹くひとよ

YOU ON THE FLUTE

You on the flute!
When you blow my flute
I'll leave
when you play enraptured
I'll be gone
leaving hurriedly
from your fingertips
from your moistened mouthpiece
I'll leave
on this lovely midnoon
for blooming flowers
for flowing waters
leaving you behind
ever farther behind
You on the flute!
When you blow my flute
when you change Sein to Sollen
that's when I'll be gone
You on the flute
Listen!

冬の噴水

噴水は
水の涸れている時が最も美しい
つめたい空間に
僕はえがくことができる
今は無いものを

僕はえがく
高くかがやくその飛揚
激しく僕に突き刺さるその落下

WINTER FOUNTAIN

A fountain is loveliest
without water
for then into that chill space
I can sketch
what doesn't meet the eye

I sketch
the high dazzling spurt
the plunge that savagely impales.

室内戯抄

1

ぱたんと
ドアがひらかれる
（僕は閉じる！）

ぱたんと
ドアが閉じられる
（僕はひらく！）

2

僕はあかりをつける
（それだけ誰か暗くなれ！）

僕はあかりを消す
（それだけ誰か明るなれ！）

3

僕は服を着る
（あずけるのだ！）

僕は服を脱ぐ
（とりもどすのだ！）

4

僕は本を読む
（うしろに誰かいる！）

僕は本を伏せる
（行った！）

INDOOR GAMES

1.

With a bang
the door is opened
    (I close it!)

With a bang
the door is closed
    (I open it!)

2.

I turn on the light
    (Someone that much darker!)

I turn off the light
    (Someone that much lighter!)

3.

I dress
    (I surrender my self!)

I undress
    (I retrieve it!)

4.

I read a book
    (Someone behind me!)

I lay it down
    (Gone!)

稲妻

稲妻が摑み出す
暗い夜の中から

眠っている工場の窓を
家と樹木を

入江の水のうすらあかりを
真菰のひとむれを

それらがもと在った場所に
ふかい闇の中に
けれどもすぐに還される

稲妻が摑み出す
暗い夜の底から
一本の野道を
歩いて行く僕を

一瞬僕の心は叫ぶ
ここへ置くな
連れて行け
放り出せ
別の場所に

LIGHTNING

Lightning reaches out
from night's murky core

Reaching for houses and trees
and sleeping factory windows
for a clump of rushes
for feeble glints of water in the cove

But it quickly returns
to the pitch dark
to the deeps that spawned it

Lightning reaches out
from night's murky depths
for that lone path through the field
for me walking on it

Instantly my heart cries out
Don't leave me here
Take me away
and discard me
somewhere else!

遠い眺め

ずっと遠く
目の限り
空と水の中へ
細まつて行つてる
岬の突端の一点
あれが僕です
突端の
そのまた突端の
岩でもない
水でもない
空でもない
在りもしない
消えもしない
あれです
あれです

A DISTANT VIEW

Far in the distance
nearly out of sight
trailing off
into sky into water
a dot at the tip of the cape
Me!
At a point
beyond that point
not rock
not water
not sky
neither lingering
nor leaving
it's me
me.

CHANSON D'AMOUR

1

不意に僕の灯りが暗くなる
僕の分もいっしょに
君が大きな灯りをともすからだ
夜が更けると　それがひどく　はっきりする

2

僕は灯りの下に立つ
うっとりとして痛ましく
僕は君の灯りを見上げる
不意に影絵が大きくのびてきて
灯りが消される
僕自身も消される
夜風の中に
あとかたもなく

3

僕は花を剪り終って
投げ出された花鋏のごときものだ
僕はつめたく黒い物体だ
けれども僕は待つ
貪婪に
僕の牙にかかる
しなやかな花の茎を

4

星がひとつともった
うまごやしの花より淡い色に
草の上はひんやりして寒い

CHANSON D'AMOUR

1.

Suddenly my lamp darkens
because you light your brighter lamp
by mine
My darkness deepens as night wears on.

2.

I stand under your lamp
wretchedly spellbound
A shadow suddenly reaches out
as I look up at you
and your light flickers away
I too am snuffed out
nothing of me left
in night's wind.

3.

I'm a cold black object
a pair of pruning shears
laid aside after clipping some flowers
yet I wait
greedily
for supple stems
to touch my blades.

4.

One star lit
its white weaker than clover
I feel chilled and cold on the grass

もうずいぶん長いことここにいたようです
僕はちょっと帰ってきましょう
帰って手さぐりで
僕の部屋の灯りをつけてきましょう
灯がついたら
すぐ僕は気づくでしょう
僕がまだここにいることを
ここにつめたい草を藉いたままでいることを
明るい灯の輪の中で
それがはっきりするでしょう
ではちよつと帰ってきます
ちよつとです

It seems I've been here awhile
I'll go home briefly
and grope for
the light in my room
Once on
I suppose I'll know
that I'm still here
stretched out on this chilling grass
Once circled by warm light
I'll know for sure
Well   I'm going home a second
just a second.

火の記憶　広島原爆忌にあたり

とある家の垣根から
蔓草がどんなにやさしい手をのばしても
あの雲をつかまえることはできない
遠いのだ
あんなに手近にうかびながら

とある木の梢の
終りの蝉がどんなに小さく鳴いていても
すぐそれがわきかえるような激しさに変る
鳴きやめたものがいっせいに目をさますのだ

町の曲り角で
田舎みちの踏切で
私は立ち止って自分の影を踏む

太陽がどんなに遠くへ去っても
あの日石畳に刻みつけられた影が消えてしまっても
私はなお強く　濃く　熱く
今在るものの影を踏みしめる

MEMORIES OF FIRE*

Hiroshima [Many Hiroshima Victims]

However far they stretch their gentle fingers
from the fence around that house
vines cannot grasp the cloud
It's very very far away
though floating so near their fingertips

However softly the last locust buzzes
on that branchtip
its hum quickly turns to violent frenzy
Whatever had fallen silent awakens as one

Stopping at a street corner
or at a grade crossing in the country
I step on my shadow

However distant the sun
however that form burned into the walk then may fade
I'll step more carefully on what shadows remain
more firmly more intently more ardently.

死　者

片びらきの鎧戸が
夜風に軋っていた
立ち止って
僕はその音を聴いた
君がちょっと出かけている時と同じだと思いながら

あれから何日経ったろう
古びた鎧戸だけが
絶え間なく軋りながら
今も君を待っているようにみえる

僕は見た
マントを翼のように鳴らして
君が帰ってくるのを
垣根づたいに這いあがり

屋根から自分の部屋へはいろうとするのを
夜風がそれを引きずり出そうとするのを
そのたびに鎧戸が開いたり閉じたりするのを
僕は立ち止って
外燈のうすらあかりで
それをみた

THE DEAD

One half-closed shutter
clatters in night wind
Pulling up
I listen to the racket and think
it's just like when you stepped out

How many days have passed since then?
Only that dilapidated shutter
clattering endlessly
seems still to wait for you

I watch
you come home
your cape flapping like wings
I watch you mount the hedge fence
and go into your room from the roof
as night winds tug the shutter
each gust opening it closing it

Pulling up
I watch
from under the feeble street light.

黒い蠅

貨車に積まれた牛たちは
首をすりつけ合い
ぼんやりと
眼をひらく

黒い蠅は
牛たちにたかりながら
ここまでいっしょにきた

貨車の中の牛たちは
自分を待ちうけている運命に向かつて
ものうげに啼く

血ぶくれのした
黒い蠅は

BLACK FLIES

Crammed into cattlecars
the cows rub heads
eyes vaguely
open

Black flies
journey
on the cattle

The cows
low gloomily
at the fate confronting them

Gorged with blood
the black flies

遠くから
貨車にゆられながら
ゆっくりした絶え間ない牛のしっぽに追われながらここまできた

この執拗で残忍な同行者は
結局どこへ行くだろう
最後に
牛たちが
ばらばらの肉塊になり
鈎にぶらさがり
やがて
鈎だけが
宙にゆれるとき

have come a long way
jostled by the train
shooed by the slow and constant swish of tails

Where do you suppose such tenacious
such merciless traveling companions will end up
when finally
the cows
become cuts of beef
hanging on hooks?
when in due course
the hooks
dangle empty in space?

風景

あかくさびた鉄の鎖が
水面から空間へのびている
水の中へ落ちこんでいる部分は
何と静かで平和だろう
そよぐ芦
歌うよしきり

けれどもみよ水から浮かんでいる部分だけが
自分で自分をみつめることができるのだ
水のおもてに
熱く灼けて身をよじりながら
そよぐ芦
歌うよしきり

SCENE

Bright rusted chains
reach from water into space
Such peace such stillness
in what lies submerged
    rustling reeds
    a singing warbler

But look!   only what soars beyond the surface
can watch itself
twisting ember hot
above the water
    rustling reeds
    a singing warbler.

寺にて

ずいぶん黒い柱である
ゆかも黒く光っている
油虫の背中さえ誰かが磨いたようだ
暮れがたの竹林が
厨の窓からすぐにつづいている
桶の水に浸けられた豆腐のように
私もひんやりと坐ってみる
郭公が鳴いている
たけのこの皮を脱ぐ音がきこえる

AT THE TEMPLE

The pillars quite black
floorboards also glistening black
even the roaches polished black

At twilight the bamboo grove
nearly touches our scullery window

I sit as cool
as beancurd soaking in the bucket
A cuckoo sighs and I hear
the sound of new bamboo   peeling.

ふるさと

みんな祭へ行つたらしい
村ぜんたいがるすのようだ
縁側の桶に
ひと握りのわらびが浸けてある
風が笛と太鼓の音をはこんでくる
午後二時の上りのけむりが
ゆつくりと列車を離れる
その影におどろいて鶏が飛び立つ
ああふるさと
祭の寿司に添えられる春菊のように
僕はいつも新鮮で孤独でありたい
（それを感じるためにこうしてかえってくるのだが）
不意に台所で柱時計が鳴る
ぜんまいのほぐれる音もきこえる
締めの足りない水栓のように
僕の眼から涙がしたたる

MY HOME TOWN*

Apparently they all went to the festival
the entire village seems deserted
A bunch of bracken soaks
in a bucket on our veranda
Sounds of flute and drum float in on the breeze
Leisurely trailing the train
smoke from the two p.m. inbound scatters shadows
A startled hen takes wing . . .
Ah my native village
I would always feel as renewed and lonely
as leaves garnishing my boxlunch sushi
(I've come back home today to know that feeling)
Suddenly the kitchen clock chimes
I hear its spring unwind as well
One tear escapes as from a tap
not quite perfectly shut.

'playing down' the orientation of the original —

冬の野にて

僕は枯草の上に坐る
石をひろつて靴の鋲を打つ
僕から離れ去ろうとするものを打つ
激しく打つ

ON A WINTER FIELD

Sitting on withered grass
I pick up a stone to hit the hobnail
I hit what would leave me
hit it hard.

若き日

僕は枯芝の上に坐っている
冬の日射しがうしろからのぞきこむ
あたたかい手を僕の肩に置く
その手は愛とかなしみにみちている

僕は思い出す
僕にやさしかった人々の手のことを
いつもふんわりとうしろから差しのべられた大きな手のことを

僕は思い出す
片意地に　ときに歯ぎしりさえしながら
いつもはらいのけたそれらの手のことを

なぜだろう？　なぜそうしたのだろう？
べつだん理由はなかったのだ

僕は起き上って外套のえりを立て
枯芝のスロープをいっさんに駈け下りる

YOUTHFUL DAYS

I sit on the brown turf
Winter sunlight peering from behind
lays warm hands on my shoulders
hands charged with love and grief

I recall
the hands of people kind to me
huge hands ever stretching gently from behind

I recall
hands I invariably brushed away
balking   at times gnashing my teeth

Why? Why act that way?
No particular reason

I stand   turn up my overcoat collar
and dash pell-mell down the withered slope.

みそさざいの歌

また田舎へ帰ってゆく
僕はひとりで帰ってゆく
冬ざれの野を小走りに鳴きながら
丘の茨の実の間から
しばらくながめていた街の夕空
けれども僕は帰ってゆく
僕を待っている
稲架の城　藁塚の砦
小さな小さなわが宇宙
夜ふけに君を目ざめさせる
風の音が僕の歌だと思ってくれ
こわれた僕の笛だと思ってくれ

THE WREN'S SONG

I'm returning to the countryside
going back home
Chirping hurriedly over withered fields
I look briefly at the city's evening sky
through briar berries on the hill
But I'm going back
they're waiting for me
those drying-rack castles those straw-mound forts
my tiny tiny world
Think of wind's roar that wakes you late at night
as my song
consider it my broken flute.

きさらぎ

子供が野遊びからかえつてきた
日が暮れて寒かつたと言う
手や足に野焼の匂いがまだのこつている
枯草や芒や茨の燃える匂いがのこつている

さて僕は
夜ふけの机によりかかつて
おもむろに自分の火を放つのだ
このこころに
このこころの枯草に

FEBRUARY*

My boy came home from playing in the fields
He said the sun went down and he felt chilled
He smelled like burnt-over fields
like burnt eulalia fronds and briars and dry grass

And now
I lean on my late-night desk
calmly lighting private fires
to my mind
to the dry grasses in my mind.

暗い絵

田舎の町の展覧会で君の昔の絵をみた。僕も住んでたことのある東京の場末の風景。灰色の空とごみごみした屋根のつらなり。——今もその向うに美しい虹がかかり、その下に大きな頭の夢が住んでるのを僕はみた。ひどく暗い色もそれらを落ちつかせるためにあり粗末な額ぶちさえもそれらが飛び去らないためにはめてあるのではないか。僕自身もまた（僕の黄色い皮膚もやせた肋も！）内部からきらめき去ろうとするもののために在るのではないか。僕はうらがなしい気持で君の暗い絵をみていた。若い女が会場の戸を閉しはじめるまで僕はみていた。

A GLOOMY PAINTING

At an exhibition in a country town I saw a picture you had painted long ago. A scene from a rundown section of Tokyo where I too had once lived. An ashen sky and rows of squalid roofs . . . I saw that beautiful rainbow hanging even now in the distance, and those ambitious dreams ensconced beneath it. I wondered whether the painting's gloomy colors did not serve to calm it down, and whether it wasn't set in a crude frame to keep it from soaring off. I too exist (both my yellow skin and my fleshless ribs) for what goes sparkling off from my innermost self.

I gazed glumly at your painting. Until a young woman began to shut up the gallery.

冬の虹

駅の陸橋をわたるとき
虹が出ていた
消えかけていたけれど美しかった
誰も気がつかなかった
教えようとしたら汽罐車の煙が吹き消した
あっというまもなかった
（人生にはこれに似た思い出がたびたびある）
改札口のところで振り返ったが
やはり見えなかった

WINTER RAINBOW

When I crossed the bridge over the tracks
a rainbow appeared
already thinning but lovely
I thought of calling it to someone's attention
when a puff of smoke from an engine scattered it
in an instant
(I often have memories like that)
I glanced back from the wicket
but of course the bow was gone.

鴨

どれくらいの時がたつたでしょう。真菰のかげから私を撃つたあの男はもういない。沼べりの林の奥の、樹の根もとに私はよこたわつていたのです。枝々を透いて、澄んだ夜空がみえます。傷口からしたたる血が、落葉にかすかな音を立てるのがわかります。はるかな、はるかな気持です。沼の水が、枯草や菱の実をうかべたまま凍つてゆくのを聴いています。百千の星が、大空の傷のようにかがやくのをみています。ああ、げに、私の負うている弾丸傷もまたひかりがかがやくようです。

MALLARD

How long has it been? The fellow who shot me from behind the rushes has left by now. Lying near the roots of a tree deep in those woods on the bank of the marsh, I watch night's crystal sky through gaps in the branches. Blood dripping from my wound makes faint sounds on crinkled leaves . . . so very far away. I listen to the marsh freezing dried grass and water chestnuts that float on its surface. I watch thousands of stars sparkle like wounds in the sky. Indeed my bullet hole seems to sparkle too.

ルナ・パークにて

草が茂っている
道は
その中に深く
しずむ

雲は
卵の形の熱さを
水の中で
抱く

噴水は
永遠に立ち上る
ベンチに
その高さだけの影を置いて

うぐいすは
自分の歌にも目ざめ
葉かげの蝸牛は
青い嵐にもねむる

おお
ここで
われら若き日
緑金の虫のように
いつもたやすく溺死した

おお
われら
ここから
すべてを割箸のように折って
踏みにじって
去る

LUNAR PARK*

Grass grows lush
The road
sinks deep
into it

Clouds
embrace
oval warmths
in the water

The fountain
rises tirelessly
laying its long shadow
over the benches

A warbler
sings itself awake
a snail with a leaf umbrella
sleeps even through the green storm

Yes
here
our youthful days
always expired with ease
like iridescent beetles

Ah
we
shall leave
here
trampling all things underfoot
snapping them like throwaway chopsticks.

つめたい風のひと吹きごとに

いちめんに芦が枯れている
芦をそめる血の色の夕焼も
かれらを燃すことはできない
つめたい風のひと吹きごとに
夕焼はうすれてゆく
入江の水のおもても芦も
だんだんに暗くなる
芦は枯れ伏しながら
そよぎながら
自分から連れ去られる血の色を思つている
つめたい風のひと吹きごとに

EACH GUST OF CHILLY WIND

All the reeds rust
Not even the blood red hue of sunset's glow
can set them afire
Each gust of chilly wind
pales evening's flush
Both the surface of the cove and the reeds
darken bit by bit
Rusting and hanging their heads
rustling in the wind
reeds ponder the blood red hues
lost to each gust of chilly wind.

十年

警報が出るたびにまっくらになった
明るいものといえば夜ぞらの銀河
燃えている市街の遠あかり
川のほとりで歯ぎしりしながら
つかみしごいた蓼の穂のつぶつぶが
水に浮くのがよく見えた
記憶の黒い布を垂れると
僕の内部は今でもすぐ同じになる
その人はまっくらやみに正坐したままで
しばらく話をつづけられた
杜子美のことを
戦乱の中でこの誠実の詩人がいかにくるしんだかを
〈三年飢えて走る荒山の道〉
〈林猿わがために清昼に啼く〉
辞して手さぐりで庭に下りたら

僕の肩にふれるものがあった
夜つゆにぬれた小さなざくろの実であった
忘れていた季節の重さを
僕はてのひらで味わった
夢のように銀河がかたむいていた
その人も蓼の穂のひとつぶのように消え去ったが
庭のざくろはまもなく青い実をつける

TEN YEARS*

Air raid sirens blackened everything
nothing bright in night skies but the Milky Way
or the distant glow of the town in flames
Gnashing my teeth on the riverbank
I often saw stripped-off smartweed spikes
on the water
I need only drop memory's ebony cloth
to relive what I felt then

Sitting square shouldered in the dark
our haiku teacher talked for some time
about Tu Fu
about how this loyal poet suffered in time of war
        "Starving three years on rugged mountain trails"
        "Gibbons weeping for me at high noon"
Saying goodbye I groped out of the yard
Something touched my shoulder
a small pomegranate wet with evening dew
I relished in my palm
the weight of that forgotten season

The Milky Way dwindled like a dream
Our teacher disappeared like the smartweed spikes
Soon the pomegranate tree will fruit again.

倒れる樹

今日大きな樹が倒されるのを見た
路傍に立ち止ってしばらく見ていた
樹は自らの成熟を知っていて
その自信と満足感の中に
ゆったりと挽き倒されるように見えた
倒れてからうちふるう枝葉にも
完成されたものの持つやすらいが眺められた

さて今はもう夜である
大きな黒い布があの傷口を覆うているであろう
そのあたり星が最も美しく輝いているだろう
夜空をわたる鳥は
樹の占めていた位置と高さで
翼にふれるつめたい空虚を感じるだろう

やがて私を挽き倒すものよ
わが生の終りにも
あのような安息と静寂があるだろうか
今日路傍で私が眺めたように
私は自らそれを感じることができるだろうか

A FELLED TREE

Today I stood by the roadside and watched
a tall tree sawed down
Aware of its maturity
the tree seemed to take the saw calmly
with a sense of satisfaction and confidence
I noted a composure born of fulfillment
even in twigs and leaves quivering on the ground

Night now   I suppose
that a huge black cloth covers those scars
that stars sparkle beautifully around them
that birds plying the night sky
feel a chilly emptiness on their wings
at the height at the spot where the tree spread out

You who will one day saw me down
at life's end
do you suppose I too might know that repose that hush?
Do you suppose I'll be capable of feeling then
what I felt today as I watched by the roadside?

僕がいつも

僕がいつも思いえがくのは
山ふかい水のしたたり
空に太陽と雲があつて
草木が生い茂つていて
岩があつて
そこからしたたる音のない音とひかり
ああ　しかし
僕は
マッチをする時の軸木のようにすばやく
蛇のようになま臭く身をよじらせて
僕は
そこを通りすぎる

I LOVE TO ENVISION

I love to envision
the trickle of water deep in the hills
sun and clouds in the sky
rampant vegetation
boulders
that drip light and noiseless sounds
And yet
whenever
I pass through such a place
I slither
smelly as a snake
swift as a struck match.

樹木たちは

小さな風が落葉を掻きわけた
その中にまだ赤い燠のようなものが交つていた
樹木たちはもう何もなくなつた枝を遠くへのべ深く差しかわし
傾き合いながら立つていた
朝がきて夜がきた
あの大きく熱くかがやくものは枝々の向う側を回り
星は（涙が流れるためでなく内側に凍るためにのみあるように）
深く差しかわしたものの間で
まばたきながらともつていた

TREES

A slight breeze scuffles through fallen leaves
mixed with something red something emberlike
Trees reach out and lean against one another
densely intermingling their empty arms
Morning comes   then evening
What had glittered brilliantly arches beyond branches
and stars (frozen eyes that shed no tears)
twinkle as they light up
among those densely intermingled arms.

僕は樹木のように

僕は樹木のように自然で安定した傾斜をもつ
僕は自分を踏みしめそして縛りつけるためのふかい根をもつ
僕は熱くもつめたくもならないためのかたい樹皮をもつ
僕は仲間と触れ合うための枝と
笑い揺らぐためのみどりの葉をもつ
僕は午後の恋人たちにやわらかな影のマットをつくり
夕方それをしまいこむための太い幹と
かれらが僕から遠のいて行くのを見送るための不変の高さをもつ
朝がた駈けこんでくる若い駿馬のような風を馴らすための
かぐわしい空気と草花と光る湖水とをもつ
僕は夢みるための青空と
考えるための夜の星と
内部でだけ抱くための年輪をもつ
僕は何ものももたないためにすべてをもつ
僕は孤りであるために全体をもつ

TREELIKE

Treelike I have a natural and a balanced bearing
deep roots for standing firm and anchoring
tough bark for avoiding heat or chill
branches for touching and being touched
green leaves for trembling with laughter
I have a thick trunk for laying a soft mat of shade
                                     over afternoon lovers
and for storing the mat when evening comes
I have unchanging height for watching the lovers leave
balmy air and flowers and a sparkling lake
for taming the young stallion wind that dashes at me mornings
I have blue skies for visions
evening stars for thought
and rings reserved for hugging my inner self
Because I have no-thing I have every-thing
because I am one I am all.

冬の鴉

びわの花が
雪のこなのように咲いている
すべての窓々にあかりがともりそめる
僕もこころもあたたかくまばたくのだ
けれども僕は
その光の輪の中へはいれない
人の世の幸福も平和も
遠くから眺めてだけ過ぎるものか
田のあぜに立つて僕は
身づくろいをすませ
やおら
羽根をのべ
くちばしをむけた方角へ
突き刺さるように
飛び去る

WINTER CROW

Loquat flowers bloom
like powdered snow
As lamps start lighting up the windows
my heart and I pulse warmly
but me
I cannot enter those lightrings
Are peace and joy in man's world
things one merely views from afar?
Standing on a paddy ridge
I finish outfitting myself
leisurely
stretch my wings   and then
as though to stab the quarter
into which I point my beak
fly off.

POEMS/1959-1965

角田寛英君に

尾道千光寺山の長い長い石段を
君はのぼる　僕は降りる
じや　さよなら　またあした

尾道千光寺山の明るい桜並木の道で
君と僕はすれ違う
忙しいかい　忙しいよ　さよならまたあした

尾道千光寺山の暗い夜の石段を
星あかりをたよりに君はのぼる
手のライトをたよりに僕は降りる
さよなら　さよならよ
もう会えない

TO TSUNODA KAN'EI*

You walk up and I walk down
that long long flight of stone steps
        on the hill at Senkō Temple in Onomichi
Well   Goodbye   See you tomorrow

We pass each other
along that cheerful road lined with cherry trees
        on the hill at Senkō Temple in Onomichi
Busy?   Yes   'Bye   Seeyoutomorrow

One dark night you walk up the stone steps
        on the hill at Senkō Temple in Onomichi
following starlight
and I walk down following my flashlight
Sayonara   Sayonara
We shall not meet again.

内部

その窓は閉ざされたままだつた
中には誰もいなかつた
机の上はきちんと片づいていた
読みさしの本が置いてあり
インクの壺はからからに乾いていた
これから何かがはじまるようにみえた
もう終つたあとかもしれなかつた
とにかくひつそりかんとしていた
壁に古びた人物像の
眼だけが大きくかがやいていた
それに追い立てられるように
窓枠のすきまから覗いていたてんとう虫は
向きをかえ脊中を二つに割つて
燃えるひかりの中へ飛び去つた

INDOORS

The window shut tight
no one in the room
On the neatly ordered desk
an opened book
the inkwell dried to sand
apparently the moment for something to start
or perhaps the wake of something complete
all in all absolutely hushed
only the eyes in that faded portrait on the wall
glitter sharply
As though accused by them
the ladybug peering in through a crack by the windowframe
turns away   parts her back
flies into burning light.

かつてあそこに

教会裏のすっかり裸になってしまった樹木の梢

かつてあそこに小鳥たちの巣があった

パイプオルガンと歌声にこたえるように

青葉若葉のきらめくあたり

一本の巣が巣からぶらさがって揺れていた

愛を運びつづける小さな者と

それを待ちこがれているより小さな者たちを心にえがきながら

私はいつもふんわりした気持で眺めていた

鞭のような枝々に星のともりはじめるあたり

かつて愛し愛される者のひとときがあったのだ

それを思い出すのはよいことだ

今私が人にも自分にもそむいて

すべての巣からはみ出されている寒さと孤独を感じるときに

ONCE THERE WAS

Once there was a bird's nest
on that now barren branchtip behind the church
Keeping time with pipe organ and choir
a piece of straw dangled from the nest
near sparkling young leaves
I always looked fondly at that nest
picturing little things bringing love in
and smaller things eagerly awaiting it
There was a time to love and be loved
near where stars begin shining on whip-like twigs
It's a comfort to recall such scenes now
when I turn against others and myself
when I feel the freeze the loneliness
of having been forced from every nest.

熊平武二さんの詩碑の前に

詩酒生涯
なんぞその響きの佳なる

詩酒生涯
なんぞその響きの悲痛なる

熊平さん
私たちは
いや私は
同じ道をおくれて歩むひとりとして
あなたの
その
暗い美しい深淵を
つまさき立つて覗きこむ
明るい五月の光と風の中に

BEFORE KUMAHIRA TAKEJI'S POETRY STELE*

—A life of poetry and wine—
  how nice!

—A life of poetry and wine—
  how sad!

Takeji
we would
or I would
as one struggling along the same Way
stand on tiptoe
in May's bright light and bright breezes
to peer into those
into your
dark and lovely deeps.

呼ぶ人

枯野のまんなかで
犬を呼んでいる
まだかえってこない
愛する者を呼んでいる

ひどく寒い日の暮れ方だ
オーバーの襟を深く立てながら
あんなに振りしぼった声で
呼ぶんだろうか
呼ばれているんだろうか
僕は

THE CALLER

Standing in the heart of a withered field
somebody calls his dog
calls a pet he loves
one who hasn't yet come home

Twilight of a bitterly cold day
I wonder if he snuggles deep into his overcoat collar
as he yells
at the top of his lungs
or could he be calling
me?

愛と死の歌

もうさよならを言いましょう
街路樹の下に落し忘れた
片っぽの黒手袋のように
私はあなたが好きだつた

濁つた水の堀割の
夕焼の
教会裏の
ピアノの
あふれてきて突き刺さるひとよ
あふれてきて突き刺さるひとよ

SONG OF LOVE AND DEATH

Let's say goodbye now
I was as fond of you
as of that single black glove
lost under a roadside tree

Behind the church
where sun's afterglow
gilds murky ditch water
your piano tunes
overwhelm and run through me
overwhelm and run me through.

死の歌

僕はまもなく死ぬだろう
僕は完全な無機物になるだろう
僕は今までもたなかった自由をもつだろう

僕は視る
僕を燃やす焔の色で

僕は語る
僕を燃やす風の音で
そして僕は

自分を抱いていた地球を
別な愛のかたちで抱く

SONG OF DEATH

Soon I'll die
and turn completely to ash
gaining a freedom I've never known

I'll see
with the hue of the flame that kindles me

I'll speak
with the sound of the blast that kindles me
and

hold with a new love
the Earth that so long held me.

夜更けの口笛

終電車が通りすぎてからしばらくして
きまって私の家の外を口笛を吹きながら行く人がある
私もいくらかききおぼえのある
トラヴィアタの一節のこともあるし
チャイコフスキィの何とかという曲のこともある
田舎の町はずれでめった人の通らない時刻である
若い人か中年かどこの誰だか分らないが
よほどおそい勤めをもった人であろう
嵐のような終電車の音に気がつかなくても
その口笛にだけには耳を澄ませることがある
きこえなくてもきこえていたような気さえする
人間は全然見知らぬ他人とでも
何かのかすかな見えないものでつながっているのだ
夜ふけの机にむかいながら心寂しい時私は
いつもそう自分に言いきかせる
同じような思いを口笛の人も

LATE NIGHT WHISTLER

Shortly after the last train
at an hour people rarely walk these outskirts of our country town
someone regularly passes my house
whistling a passage from La Traviata
or some tune or other by Tchaikovsky
pieces that even I am faintly familiar with
I don't know if he's young or middle aged or who or where he's from
probably someone whose job keeps him late
When I miss the roar of the last train
his whistling often catches my ear
and I find myself hearing him even if he isn't there
When I sit alone at my desk late into the night
I constantly remind myself
that faint invisible bonds relate people
even total strangers
I wonder if the whistler has similar thoughts

私の家の灯に抱いてくれているのではないかしら

十二月の夜ふけのことであった
ききなれたその口笛の音がとぎれて
ふいに自転車の呼鈴を鳴らす音がした
「もし　もし　自転車が出たままですよお宅のではありませんか」
子供のしまい忘れた自転車を
私も家の者もうっかりしていたのである
あわてて外に出てみたがどちらの方角へ消えたか
もう口笛の音はきこえなかった
クリスマスも近い晴れた美しい夜空で
オリオンが南へ大きく傾いていた
つめたくぬれた自転車の呼鈴を
口笛の人をまねて私も鳴らしてみた

when he sees the light on in my room?

Late one December evening
that familiar whistle broke off
and a bicycle bell surprised me
"Say, there's a bike here. Is it yours?"
The children had forgotten
to bring in the bicycle
I hurried outside (but where had he gone?)
his whistling had already faded away
Orion inclined sharply toward the south
in a beautifully crisp late December sky
Mimicking the whistler
I whirred the bell on our cold and dewy bike.

歌　唱

まつすぐに顔を上げて
歌を唱うこどもたち
窓の外に立つている一本の樹木のように
僕は僕の枝と葉を揺すつてあげよう

大きく眼をひらいて
歌を唱うこどもたち
僕はピアノにむかう十本の指と二本の足のように
落ちついて焦りながら
その大切な部分を一しよに押えていてあげよう

歌を唱うこどもたち
美しい美しいものたち
花瓶の花にかくれている一ぴきの虻のように
僕は早くここから飛び去ろう
その短かい最後のひとふしの終らぬうちに

SINGING

Hold your heads high
singing children!
I'll sway my leaves and limbs for you
like that tree outside the window

Open your eyes wide
singing children!
I'll work out with you the vital parts
hurrying calmly along
like those fingers and feet at the piano

Beautiful beautiful creatures
you singing children!
I'll leave before you finish your last brief song
quick as that horsefly
hiding among flowers in the vase.

僕は涙もなくて

僕は涙もなくて
涙の多い歌をうたう
僕は愛も夢もなくて
愛と夢の歌をうたう
僕は満ちあふれることもなくて
のこされた干潟をうたう
僕は光る種子もやわらかな土壌もなくて
ひらき匂う花をうたう
詩よ　美しいものよ
ペン軸からインク壺にころがり落ちる
ペンさきのように残酷なものよ

TEARLESS

Tearless
I write poems full of tears
loveless and dreamless
I write poems full of love and dreams
never having been fulfilled
I write of mudflats deserted by the sea
with neither shining seeds nor soft soil
I write of flowers reeling in fragrance
Poetry   beautiful thing!
heartless as that penpoint
lost to my inkwell.

人生

樹木や草花はひかりの中に揺れさざめき
空の雲は立ちどまつてその影を
かがやく噴水やまるい芝生の上に置いていた

幌をふかく垂れこめた乳母車の幼児のように
私はねむりながらそこを通りすぎた

ああわが父母わが妻わが子わが友がき
すべての愛と平和にみちたものたち
私は今一番おそくともる星のように
閉ざされて行く世界にむかつて眼をひらく
まだ終りきらない小鳥のさえずりを抱いて
暮れなやむ一本の樹木のようにかげふかく
私は私の言葉を語る

MY LIFE

Trees and flowers flicker crisply in the light
A cloud pulls up to lay its shadow
over the gleaming fountain over a round patch of grass

I've passed through here asleep
an infant in a buggy with the hood down

My parents my wife my children my friends
those filled with all love and peace . . .
I open my eyes now to a world being shut
as though I were the last star to shine
Cherishing what bird songs remain
I speak my words in deep shade
a lone tree loath to merge with dusk.

人生

私の生れた村
私の幼年時代

白い道が一本
回虫のようによじれのびている
午後の太陽がかがやき
家や森や林は
その形の影を身近く引き寄せる

ああかの日の美しい渇き
見えない存在への怖れとあこがれ

何ものの痛みであるか疲れであるか
飴売りの笛よりも遠く細長くふるえ
古娘の糸切歯よりもひそやかに
年若い行商人の薬指の指輪のように光りながら
今私を通りすぎて行くものは

MY LIFE

The village where I was born
my childhood

A single white road
unwinds like a roundworm
Under the glittering afternoon sun
houses the wood the grove
draw in their silhouettes

Ah the lovely thirsts of those days
the awe of the longing for realities beyond the eye

Whose weariness is this? whose pain?
Trembling more remote more pinched than the candyman's flute
harder to see than a spinster's eyeteeth
glittering like the rings on a young peddler's finger
. . . what passes by me now?

道

涙しながらあるいてきた道
私ひとりの道
私ひとり自分の影を踏みながら
あるいてきた道

誰もいない
誰の声もしない
夏の野原の虫捕りの子らのように
みんな遠くへ散らばった
しんかんとして太陽のきらめく
真夜中のようなまひる

誰も私を呼ばない
誰も私のありかを知らない

どこからともなく
私はきた
どこへともなく
私はあるいてきた
私自身にさえそむいてきた

私は誰をも呼ばぬ
私は誰をも探さぬ
私は呼ぶただひとりの私
私は探すただひとりの私

わが妻もわが名を呼ばぬ
わが子もわが影を探さぬ
私は寒い
自分の肋骨をへし折つて燃やすほどに
自分の影の中に深くわが手をひたすほどに

MY WAY

The path I've trekked in tears
my own Way
the path I've walked alone
trampling my shadow

No one here
no one speaks
everyone scattered
like children chasing bugs in summer fields
Sun glistening in exquisite silence
high noon like midnight

Nobody calls me
nobody knows where I am

I've come
from no place in particular
walked
toward no place in particular
come despite myself

I call to no one
search for no one
I call only to my solitary self
search only for my solitary self

My wife doesn't even call my name
nor do my children look for me
I'm cold
cold enough to shatter my ribs and burn them
to burrow my hands deep in my shadow

もし誰かが私を呼ぶとき
もし誰かが私を探すとき
私はこたえ得るだろうか
草の中にまだ暮れなやむ石のひかりで
日のすっかり落ちたあとの
荒野を吹きすぎてゆく風の言葉で

If someone calls me
if someone asks for me
could I answer with a glint from that weed-held stone
loath to lose itself in dusk?
with wind's words rumbling across the wilds
in sunset's darkening wake?

踏切にて

かたんと遮断機が降りて
私を立止まらせる場所
うらうらとした春の日の
私の思いを切断する場所
麦が青く菜畑が黄いろく
電車が遠い潮騒を連れてやってくる
ああ今二本のレールとともに光り走って来て
私に突き刺さるものは何だろう
そらまめの花の黒い眼のように物言わず
亡霊のようにそこにむらがつて
私をみつめているのは誰ですか

AT A GRADE CROSSING*

This is where the clatter of the crossing gate
stopped me in my tracks
the place that put an end to my pleasure
on this joyfully sunny spring day
barley green   rape fields golden
the train ushering in surf's distant roar . . .
What now would run me through
dashing at me   shining along the rails?
What stares me down
crowding the tracks like ghosts
mute as the black eyes on soramame petals?

私のうたは

私のうたは真夜中
水道の蛇口からもれるしたたり
私のうたは誰もいない片隅で
ともしびも皿も茶碗も眠つた頃はじまる
涙のように愛の言葉のように
私のうたははじまる
私のうたはあなたの知らない
あなたの締め忘れたところからはじまる
ああ長く暗くつめたい夜
長く暗くつめたい夜の
自分を凍らせるものにむかつて
私のうたははじまる

MY POEMS

My poems
trickle from a midnight tap
arise in lonely corners
when lamps and cups and dishes have gone to sleep
My poems begin
like tears like words of love
starting from places you do not know
from places you've forgotten to shut
This long   black   chilly night!
My poems arise
in answer to what freezes me
on long   black   chilly nights.

夜明けの樹木　或る幻想から

誰も見ていない今
何の物音もない今
まだともる星を遠く
枝と葉のさざめきをかかげて
幹は深く静かに爽やかである
ああその固い樹皮に内蔵される
年輪をのぞき見て
疾くゆるく
光る小さな眼のように
露のたまが走り去る

TREE AT DAWN:

a fantasy

No one watches now
nothing breathing
stars still flicker in the distance
the trunk profoundly serene and vital
its leaves and twigs raising a clamor
Beads of dew slip down its side
softly   swiftly
and peer like little glittering eyes
into year rings
deep within tough bark.

午前

汽車のけむりが
ゆっくりと
むぎばたけの上にきて消える
白いマスクのような
汽車のけむりの影が
農家の庭の鶏たちを驚かせる
小さな駅と駅をつないで
北へ北へ向かう私設鉄道
もう二度とは見れないだろうと
ぼんやり窓枠にもたれて眺めていた
あの早春の山峡の村々

FORENOON

Smoke from the engine
lazes over barley fields
then disappears
Shadows from the smoke
shaped like white masks
startle chickens in farmyards
The private railroad stretching northward
connects one toy station with another
Thinking I'm unlikely to see them again
I lean vacantly against the windowjamb and gaze
at the hamlets in this greening gorge.

砂　湯　　湯原温泉

夜明けの水銀灯がともっている
湯気の霞の中から
妖精のような裸体がうかぶ
三保の松原の天女は
羽衣をとられてから人間に成りさがったが
ここでは宿の格子縞の浴衣をぬいで
それからおもむろに天女になる

SAND BATH∗

Yubara Spa

Dawn's mercury lamps aglow
fairy-like nudes
float up through steamy mists
Loss of her magic robes once humbled
the nymph of Miho-no-Matsubara into humanhood
but now guests doff the spa's checkered yukata
and turn serenely into nymphs.

勝山駅にて

上りの汽車を待っている
ぼくの手のたばこ
まだくゆっている
ぼくの半日

空はよく晴れていて暑く
プラットホォムに下りてくる
雲の影もない

遠くの街道を
黒びかりのする美作牛を追うて
若い女があるいてゆく

AT KATSUYAMA STATION*

Waiting for the inbound train
my cigarette
smolders on
half my day

Sky is very clear and hot
not a single cloud shadow
visits the platform

A young woman walks down
the distant highway
driving a glossy black cow.

雉

ここの熊笹
ここの茂みの中
ぼくは逃げる
追跡者の速度に合せて
静かに　速く

追跡者の爪の届く前に
ぼくには飛び立つ空がある
そのひろがりを頭の上に感じながら
ぼくは逃げる　静かに早く

ここの熊笹
ここの茂みの中
ぼくは逃げる
あぁ飛び立つ

青空に吊りあげられる
その一瞬の
自分の重さを想いながら

THE PHEASANT *

I flee
into this bamboo grass
this thicket
a step ahead of my pursuer
calmly   quickly

I have the sky to wing into
before his claws reach me
Aware of the blue spreading out above
I flee   calm and quick

I flee
into this bamboo grass
this thicket
and take wing
feeling in the instant
I'm borne up by blue skies
all my weight.

芦の歌

街のざわめきが
気の早い蜂の羽音のようにきこえてくる
ここに私は立っています
牛の角に似た新しい芽を
さざなみの面にうつしながら

私は何を考えよう何を想おう
私につらくつめたかった日のことか
私をいつもそよがせる未来のことか
水にひたした足はまだつめたくて
頭だけがだんだん熱くなる

ああ今影とともにさざめき連れて
遠い残雪のようにかがやいて

かもめのひと群れが過ぎて行く
大空にかれらの翼がつくり出す
さざなみのひかりと音の中を

SONG OF THE REED

Town's commotion fills my ears
like the buzz of restless bees
I stand here
my green horn-like buds
mirrored on wavelets

What to ponder? what to think about?
the days that so bitterly chilled me?
the future that forever makes me tremble?
Soaking feet still freeze
only my head gradually warms

Leading away the hubbub   pulling shadows
and glinting like snow left on far-off peaks
gulls glide through light ripples   *now*   through sound ripples
their wings have left in the sky.

元　旦

雪と霜と氷を踏んで
われら今年の第一歩を署名する
8760時間を今の一瞬にこめて
わが心に充たす火薬
わが手の指にかかる撃鉄
ああ雪と霜と氷を踏んで
われら狩人にしてかつ獲物
われら追う者にしてかつ追われるもの

NEW YEAR'S DAY

Tramping over snow and frost and ice
we autograph our first step into the new year
cramming 8760 hours into a single moment
     gunpowder packed into my mind
     my finger on the trigger
Yes tramping over snow and frost and ice
we the hunters we the game
the pursuers   the pursued.

或る晴れた日に

あまりにも気持のよい秋晴なので
乗合自動車の一区間だけを
わざわざ降りてあるくのである

先ず電柱を風除けとして
たばこの火をつけ終る
とたんに方角をうしない
再びもと来た方へとあるいている
周囲は青く低い山なみで
前後は同じような街衢がひろがり
すでに東西を弁じ難いのである

小さな橋を見れば
その橋を渡つてみたくなり
芦や真菰の花がそよいで居れば
そのほとりにたたずむ

水の面は常に暗く濁つていて
影をひたしに来るとんぼも見あたらない

美しき婦人の路次に入るを見れば
ついそのあとに蹤いて行き
ポケットの定期入れを手にしながら
あたかも家をたずねている者のごとくに装うのである
しかしおおむねそこは袋小路であつて
いずこか美しき婦人の姿は在らず
金木犀だけがことさらよく匂つているのである

空は漠々たる雲に閉ざされ
私は今ははや
水晶と山葡萄を探しに来て
仲間にはぐれた少年のごとくに孤独なのである

ON A SUNNY DAY *

It's such a pleasantly clear autumn day
I decide to get off the bus a stop early
and walk home

First I light up a cigarette
in the lee of a utility pole
Having already lost my bearings
I find myself walking in the direction from which I came
surrounded by wavy green knolls
identical crossroads ranging before and behind
no longer able to tell east from west

Seeing a little bridge
I'd like to cross it
seeing rushes in bloom and reeds stirring
I'd like to stand next to them awhile
pond water darkly roiled
and no dragonfly soaking its shadow

Seeing a beautiful lady enter some lane
I'd like to fall in behind her and
bus pass in hand
act as though I'm looking for a house
but the lane would be a dead end
no beautiful lady anywhere
only a fragrant daphne exuding its special pungence

Sky shut out by endless clouds . . .
by now I feel as isolated
as that boy who wandered from friends
while hunting for crystal and wild grapes.

八月の歌　水の想い

さかまき揺らぐ髪の毛で
私は何者をもとらえない
泡立ち躍る言葉で総てを
ただ洗い清めながら私は
「現代」から「未来」へ
「現象」から「思考」へ
溶けて行く　流れて行く
ああ壮麗な夏の光りを
内部に深く屈折させながら
静かである
遙かである
私の心は今

AUGUST

water's thoughts

I entangle no one
in my billowing ringlets
I merely wash all things clean
with words that roil and dance
melting   flowing
from Present to Future
from Phenomenon to Thought
Bending summer's glorious radiance
deep into my self
my mind now turns
calm
distant.

僕は生きられる

僕は生きられるだろう
僕は生きる
ただひとりでも僕は生きる
枯草の中で僕をつまづかせる
石のような
自分の生を確かめて

僕は生きられるだろう
僕は生きる
朝のかまどの火のように
白菜の肌を舐めまわす

僕は生きられるだろう
僕は生きる
肉と骨から完全に分離されて
夜ふけの皿の煮凝のように

僕は生きられるだろう
僕は生きる
中途でよじれちぎれながら
物をつかんでいる
枯れた蔓草のように

I CAN MAKE IT *

I can make it
I'll survive
like flames on the morning range
that lick the tough Chinese cabbage stalk

I can make it
I'll survive
like the aspic from my midnight snack
severed completely from flesh and bone

I can make it
I'll survive
like a withered vine
clinging doggedly somehow
though partially mangled and torn

I can make it
I'll survive
survive alone
testing life
the way that rock made me stumble
on the withered turf.

返り花

返り花　ほのかに白く咲く
太陽は　遠くあゆみ去り
蔓草は石をめぐつて枯れ
忘られた人として　今花ひらく

我等の人生も　かくあらしめよ
誰か　この花を見るべき
誰か　ここにたたずむべき
遠い日の恵みにむかい
ひかり静かに寂び明かる

IN ITS SECOND BLOOMING

A flower in its second blooming blossoms a faint white
Sun saunters into the distance
a vine withers round a rock
but that flower blooms now like someone forgotten

O renew our lives like this!
Someone   should watch this flower
someone   should linger here . . .
light mellows softly shimmers softly
into the bounties of far-off days.

夜の狐

夜ふけの机に向かつて
狐の声をききながら
煮凝のように
黙っている

実だけあかい壺の南天
机の下に棲む風
あなたの投げてくれた
雪つぶての中から
小石が出てきたような
そういう思いである

夜の狐は
何と悲しいスピードだろう
ひと声はつい近くで

すぐつぎのひと声は二百メートルも先き
遮断機を上げつぱなしの田舎みちを
私も今
飢えた狐と一しよに走っている
月光のようにまつしぐらに

EVENING FOX *

Late at night
I sit at my desk
silent as aspic
listening to a fox

I think
of our potted nandina only its berries red
of drafts ensconced under my desk
of those pebbles
in the snowball
you tossed to me

That evening fox
what deplorable speed!
One bark near and the very next one
two hundred meters beyond

I run now
with the famished fox
over a country lane its crossing gate up
all out   like moonlight.

光る人　スポーツ詩断片

跳躍する人よ
あなたは「悪」を蹴るように
地球を蹴る
蹴った
飛んだ
あなたはあなただけにある
実在を摑む
白い雲のやわらかさ
大空の青の深さ
瞬間あなたを支えている
空間のエーテル
ぼくらは息を呑んで
あなたの落下を受けとめる
無数の熱い砂だ

泳ぐ人よ
あなたは囚われの魚のように
すばやく　なめらかに
かえってぼくらを囚えている
ぼくらの絶叫のこだまが
あなたの水しぶきで返ってくる
その一つぶ一つぶに
口を開けたぼくらの
顔・顔・顔もとじこめて

THE TALENTED

from a poem on athletes

1.

Long jumper!
You stomp the board
hard enough to stamp out vice
Airborne
with a footplant
your hands grasp realities
that exist for you alone
The weightlessness of white clouds
the solidity of sky's blue
suspend you fleetingly
in the spacious ether
We gasp
and become the countless grains of heated sand
that soften your landing . . .

2.

Swimmer!
Like a fish in an aquarium
you captivate us
nimbly   slickly
As our cheers resound
from your spray
each bead of water
captures face after face after face
mouths agape . . .

登攀者よ
あなたは背中に負うた
愛と孤独と
勇気と力の重さを知る
あなたは太陽の明るさと
霧の深さと
心のザイルの短さを知る
あなたの打ちこむピッケルが
あなたが自分の為に作る足場が
大きな意味のひろがりを持つのを知る

3.

Climber!
You know how strength and courage
love and loneliness
weight your shoulders
You know sun's dazzle
fog's depths
the shortness of mind's rope
You know the huge range of consequence
in your toeholds
in the pitons you drive.

海沿いの町　　呉線にて

汽車のとまっている間
波の音がよみがえる
駅の裏山の
松風も法師蟬も
かすかである

汽車の窓枠に
誰かのたべのこしたアイスクリームのように
無惨に溶けて
しずくを垂らしている
私の半生

そのしずくのひとつぶひとつぶに
映っている夕焼

プラットホームの端っこを
蟹が一ぴき
ゆっくりと歩いている
夕焼より夾竹桃の花よりあかい
その爪を
せい一ぱい振りかざして

SEASIDE TOWN*

on the Kuré Line

The roar of waves returns
when the train stops
Both wind in the pines and cicadas
on the hill behind the station
seem fainter

Half my life
melts pitifully
trickling away drop by drop
like the partly-eaten ice cream bar
left on a windowledge in the coach

sunset mirrored
in every single drop

A lone crab
crawls leisurely
along the lip of the platform
brandishing with all its might
claws redder than sunset
redder than oleanders.

長い不在

かつては熱い心の人々が住んでいた
風は窓ガラスを光らせて吹いていた
窓わくはいつでも平和な景をとらえることができた
雲は輪舞のように手をつないで青空を流れていた
ああなんという長い不在
長い長い人間不在
一九六五年夏
私はねじれた記憶の階段を降りてゆく
うしなわれたものを求めて
心の鍵束を打ち鳴らし

GONE SO LONG

Once people with burning hearts lived here
and breezes brightened windowpanes
Once windows framed peaceful scenes
and clouds linked as though dancing drifted through the blue
Oh   they've been gone so long
the people   gone so very long
Summer 1965
I descend that unforgettable spiral staircase
searching what was lost
jangling the keyring in my mind.

APPENDICES

APPENDIX I: CHRONOLOGY

1914	October 27: born the second son of Kinoshita Tsuneichi and Aya, in Miyuki Village, Hiroshima Prefecture.
1920	July 22: father killed by a milling machine in his store.
1921	April: enters Iwanari Primary School.
1922	August 3: mother marries Tsuneichi's younger brother Itsu, a pharmacist.
1927	April: enters prefectural middle school in nearby Fuchū.
1932	March: graduates from Fuchū Middle School; April: enters Waseda Academy in Tokyo to study French literature.
1935	April: enters School of Pharmacy in Nagoya; September 15: stepfather, Itsu, dies of tuberculosis.
1938	March: obtains license in pharmacy.
1939	October: first collection of poetry, COUNTRY TABLE, published privately.
1940	April: COUNTRY TABLE shares Sixth BUNGEI HANRON poetry prize; September: second book, THE HOUSE WHERE I WAS BORN.
1944	January: marries Umeda Miyako.
1945	October 29: daughter Akiko born.
1946	July: third collection, SONGS OF OLD.
1949	January 14: son Junji born; June: fourth collection, LATE SUMMER; July: fifth book LATE SPRING.
1955	July: sixth collection, SELECTED POEMS FOR CHILDREN; November: seventh collection, JUVENILE POEMS.
1956	July: first haiku collection, SOUTHWIND SKETCHES.
1958	January: eighth poetry collection, FLUTE PLAYER.
1959	May: Hiroshima Poets' Association established, chairman for four years; member of Japan Poets' Club and Association for Modern Japanese Poetry; July: second haiku collection, DISTANT THUNDER.
1961	Formation of Hiroshima Haiku Association; edits first issue of its

journal; member of Haiku Poets' Association.

1962   Commissioned by Japan National Railways to write verse for its centennial brochure.

1965   July: writes last poem, "Gone So Long," at request of CHŪGOKU NEWSPAPER to commemorate twentieth anniversary of atomic bombing of Hiroshima; August 4: dies from cancer of the colon; November: COLLECTED POETRY published in Tokyo.

1966   January: COLLECTED POETRY wins Eighteenth Yomiuri Literary Award for free-verse poetry and haiku.

APPENDIX II: TEENAGE POEMS

LONELY GROVE
I'm a tree now rooted to this spot
Untroubled
I give the far off skies my care.

OCTOBER
An apple at the tip of her white fingers
on it the clear glass of a brick building

in which I sit days on end
reading my book by a window
that sponge on the table
soaking up all I feel

My fingers turn page after page
each blank.

A DAPHNE
Unable to keep my fingertips from hoarding
those pungent daphne aromas

I find myself a lad back home
basking in the sun
against our storehouse wall.

THE WHARF

1.

A warship rusts at the wharf
One by one
blue sailors wander into the distance
over the sea.

2.

So lonely
the wharf's wind-driven lights
sidle up to me.

3.

A blind woman
drowns herself in utter silence
Moon
raises a white hand through the gloom.

4.

When I walk the wharf alone
I soon find
ancient blue Spanish stamps
pasted all across
my forehead.

APPENDIX III: NOTES

15.   yukata: Literally bathrobe; cotton kimono-like garment worn after a bath, to bed, or for relaxation on summer evenings.

21.   salvia (sarufuia or sarubia), Salvia officinalis: Aromatic herb of the mint family imported from southern Europe; type of sage. Leaves used to season Western foods; seeds for beverage or flour. Summer associations.

21.   daphne (mokusei), Osmanthus fragrans/daphne odora: Evergreen reaching a height of nine feet; exudes powerful aroma in late autumn. Sometimes called gin-mokusei (with white flowers).

27.   yomogi (mugwort, wormwood), Artemisia princeps (or indica): Also called mochigusa. Perennial aromatic herb of the chrysanthemum family; sprouts come up when the last snow melts, blooms in autumn. Appears in very early Japanese poetry. Leaves used in cooking account for associations with foods mother makes.

31.   sour sorrel (sukanpo), Oxalis acetosella: Popular name for suiba; related to buckwheat, smartweed families. In springtime children peel the skin from the stem and eat it raw; used as greens in salads.

33.   shiso (beefsteak plant), Perilla frutescens or crispa: Aromatic annual imported from China. Fragrant leaves a delicate purple; used to color pickled food. Usually has summer associations.

33.   ruby plums (yusuraume), Prunus tomentosa: Member of the rose family, imported from China; grows to nine feet. Very sweet red plums ripen in June among fresh green leaves; the fruit a favorite target of children.

47.   daphne: See page 21.

47.   red . . . ticket: In prewar days, red signified third class, the cheapest way to travel.

51. my bucket: Part of the traditional ritual during a visit to a grave includes dipping a libation of water from a pail and pouring it over the tombstone.

53. Hinomisaki: A cape and village on the Japan Sea, extreme western tip of Shimane Peninsula, Shimane Prefecture, due north of Hiroshima City. Site of celebrated lighthouse which, at 128 feet, was once the tallest man-made structure in Japan—a national monument.

57. eulalia (susuki), Miscanthus sinensis: Native of East Asia; resembles pampas grass (Cortaderia sellona). Appears in Japanese poetry from early times; associated with autumn.

63. citron (yuzu), Citrus junos: Chinese lemon; long thorns, grows to twelve feet. Very tart, exudes a pungent odor in late autumn. Skin of the citron is bumpy, its shape resembling the female breast.

67. squash/millet (kabocha/kibi): Both plants mature in autumn; they accordingly frame the poem with an anticipated fruition that contrasts with the static ennui of the scene.

73. citron: See page 63.

97. mochi: Rice pounded into a viscous mass, then formed into balls or cakes. Sometimes toasted. Associated especially with New Year's festivities.

141. burned into the walk: Refers to the shape of a human being etched on the sidewalk in front of the Sumitomo Bank; the person was vaporized by the atomic blast over Hiroshima.

153. sushi: Bite sized rice patty topped with relish and raw fish, shellfish, and the like.

161. burnt-over fields (noyaki): Custom since ancient times—controlled burning of weeds and withered grass in late winter. Facilitates growth of spring grasses, thus suggesting potentiality and hope.

169. Lunar Park: The foreign name implies a Western-style park; in this case, not a formal garden but an amusement park with rides and concessions.

173. smartweed spikes (tade no ho), Polygonum hydropiper: Sometimes called water pepper; juice used in summer to prevent insect bites. Symbol of the passing of summer, coming of autumn.

187. Tsunoda Kan'ei: Amateur poet friend of Kinoshita, director of programs on the arts for Japan Broadcasting Company (NHK), Onomichi. Arranged radio broadcasts Kinoshita made on Japanese poetry; died of a cerebral hemorrhage at forty.

187. Senko Temple: Buddhist temple of a "thousand lights," high on a hill overlooking Onomichi harbor. Shares the hilltop with a park and the transmitter and studios of Japan Broadcasting Company (NHK), Onomichi.

187. Onomichi: Inland Sea port city in Hiroshima Prefecture, some sixty miles east of Hiroshima city. Population ca. 100,000; famed since the 15th century as commercial and trading center.

193. Kumahira Takeji: Regional poet, Hiroshima area; inscription on his poetry stele is in Chinese. At the dedication of this stele, Kumahira rejected the ritually correct water oblation and used wine instead.

217. soramame (fava or horse bean), Vicia faba: Perennial cultivated in East Asia since ancient times; the large beans turn black as they mature.

225. Yubara Spa: Hot springs in northwestern Okayama Prefecture, adjacent to the border of Tottori Prefecture and due north of Okayama City. Used as a spa since the 11th century; some 300,000 visit annually.

225. Miho-no-Matsubara: Situated on a sandbar jutting into Suruga Bay near the city of Shimizu in Shizuoka Prefecture; famed since ancient times for its view of Mt. Fuji, due north. Site of the legend of the feathered robe (hagoromo), in which an angel could not immediately return to heaven because her magic robe was stolen while swimming in the area.

225. yukata: See page 15.

227. Katsuyama: Town in the northwestern section of Okayama Prefecture, population ca. 20,000; former castletown on the Izumo Road. Famous for agricultural products, including cows.

229. bamboo grass (kumazasa), Sasa albo-marginata: Dries up in late fall and turns whitish. Hillside habitat.

235. lost my bearings: Kinoshita's extremely poor sense of direction frequently caused him to get lost, even within a block or two of his home.

235. daphne: See page 21.

239. Chinese cabbage (hakusai), Brassica pekinesis: Sometimes called white rape; imported during last half of 19th century from China. A hardy plant, it flourishes in cold climates. Associated with winter.

243. nandina (nanten), *Nandina domestica*: Winter plant, evergreen of the barberry family growing to height of six feet. Red Berries develop in late fall; leaves redden during the coldest part of winter. If only the berries are red, the time is early winter or late autumn.

249. Kuré Line: Runs between Hiroshima City and Itozaki through Kuré and along the Inland Sea via Takehara and then through Mihara. Kuré a famous naval base on the southeast edge of Hiroshima Bay.

249. oleander (kyōchikutō), *Nerium indicum*: A late summer flower; resembles the rosebay, sometimes identified as phlox, the "starfire" (*Phlox paniculata*). Hot summer weather causes flowers to droop, giving the impression they are weary of blooming.

APPENDIX IV: CONTENT OF THE COLLECTIONS

Titles in brackets signify poems published in earlier collections and reprinted; unless in brackets, poems with the same title are separate works. Starred titles (*) signify poems, or an independent part of a composite poem, included in this collection.

1. COUNTRY TABLE 「田舎の食卓」

October 1939; 67 pp. plus index; 23 poems

PART I: MEMORIAL TREES ALONG THE ROAD

*Portrait of the City, On a Sun-washed Train, June Chanson, Passing Shower, *Afternoon Letter, Summer's End, Fresh Autumn Lyric, The Sloth, *The Fingers of a New Season, *Songs of Early Spring

PART II: COUNTRY TABLE

*Squall, Bonjour, Summer Sketchbook, Forenoon, Sleep, The House Where I Was Born, *Village: fragments, *Country Table, *A Lad, Soirée, Family, Autumn Song, *Autumn's Edge: fragments

2. THE HOUSE WHERE I WAS BORN 「生れた家」

September 1940; 60 pp. plus index; 30 poems

*One Day in the City, Spring, *At an Inn, *Evening, *Going Home, Late Spring Flute, Shower, *At a Country Barbershop, Night Wind, Late Spring, The Village, *L'ESPOIR, *The House Where I Was Born, En Route, Revenge, After Dinner Songs, *Songs of Old: fragments, High Noon in Summer, Viper, Blanks in Summer Notebooks, Lonely Bookworm, Summer Day, *Logging, Mémoire, Supper, *One Day of a Journey, Little Port Town, *An Autumn Afternoon, After Dinner Songs, The Field

3. SONGS OF OLD 「昔の歌」
   July 1946; 62 pp.; 24 poems, 11 of which are new

[The Field], [Spring], [A Lad], [Passing Shower], [Late Spring Flute], [Late Summer—part of "Soirée"], Daily Solitude, Grove, School, [The Village], Wheat Harvest, Seashore Town, Tardy, [Summer Day—retitle of "High Noon in Summer"], [Sleep], [Blanks in Summer Notebooks], [Logging], [Songs of Old], Lying on Fresh Grass, [Little Port Town], *Visit to a Grave, *Hinomisaki Village, *At Hinomisaki Village, *Youthful Days

4. LATE SUMMER 「晩夏」
   June 1949; 22 pp.; 9 poems, 8 of which are new

Ants, *Late Summer, Notes on Early Autumn, [Wild Flowers—from "Scenes from an Autumn Sketchbook"], Autumn Grass, *Autumn Day, *Night School Student, *At a Train Station, Winter

5. LATE SPRING 「晩春」
   July 1949; 47 pp., half devoted to poems by Fujifuchi Kinya; Kinoshita's poetry runs from page 6 through page 21; 12 poems, 7 of which are new

[Ants], The House, Fragments, Daily Chore, [Shower—retitle of "Passing Shower"], Grove, [Autumn Grass], [Autumn Day], The Heights, [At a Train Station], *The Old House, Late Spring

6. JUVENILE POEMS 「児童詩集」
   November 1955; 26 pp.; 21 poems

Meadowlark's Nest, Mountain Path, Night on the Countryside, Afternoon at the Chalet, Train Smoke, The Rainbow and the Snail, Interurban in Spring, Katydid, Bamboo Thicket, All in a Row, Memories, *The Distant Town, Heating the Bathwater, A Quiet Evening, One Day in the Kitchen, Hide and Seek, Apples, City Shower, *Path through the Fields, Little Harbor Town, Christmas Night

264

7. POEMS FOR CHILDREN 「子供のための詩抄」

June 1955 (compiled after the above manuscript); 10 pp.; 10 poems, 3 of which are new

[Apples], [Christmas Night], *Horizontal Bar, [Katydid], [Path through the Fields], [Afternoon at the Chalet], My Father, [Little Harbor Town], *Spring Bell, [Late Summer]

8. FLUTE PLAYER 「笛を吹くひと」

January 1958; 100 pp. with index plus an introduction by Ibuse Masuji; 38 poems, 34 of which are new, plus reportage on Hiroshima

PART ONE: WINTER FOUNTAIN
*The Trail, The Country, *Southwind, *I Turn to Vapor, *You on the Flute, *Winter Fountain, *Indoor Games, *Lightning, *Two Distant Views, *CHANSON D'AMOUR, *Memories of Fire: Hiroshima, *The Dead, The Quotidian Seat, *Black Flies, The Bank, *Four Scenes

PART TWO: SHARING THE SKY: REPORTAGE ON HIROSHIMA

PART THREE: NIGHT SCHOOL STUDENT
Morning, [Late Summer], Spring Valley, [Wild Flowers], [Night School Student], [At a Train Station], *At the Temple, Autumn Day, *My Home Town

PART FOUR: A FELLED TREE
*On a Winter Field, *Youthful Days, *The Wren's Song, *February, *A Gloomy Painting, *Winter Rainbow, *Mallard, Mountain Inn, Adolescence, *Lunar Park, *Each Gust of Chilly Wind, *Ten Years, *A Felled Tree

APPENDIX V: INDEX OF TITLES

APPENDIX VI: INDEX OF FIRST LINES

OAKLAND UNIVERSITY PUBLICATIONS: ASIA

ASIAN POETS IN TRANSLATION: JAPAN

Four generations of poets spanning the transitional years from the 1930s to 1980.

TREELIKE: THE POETRY OF KINOSHITA YŪJI. This translation by Robert Epp of UCLA has been awarded the Friendship Fund Prize for Japanese Literary Translation and has been selected for the UNESCO Collection of Representative Works. Published jointly with the University of Michigan Center for Japanese Studies.

A STRING AROUND AUTUMN: SELECTED POEMS 1952-1980. By Ōoka Makoto, winner of the Rekitei, Mugen, Yomiuri, and Kikuchi Kan prizes. Japanese Poet in Residence, Oakland University, Fall 1981. Preface by Donald Keene.

Poet's reading, with alternating English translations, available on cassette.

DEVIL'S WIND: A THOUSAND STEPS. Booklength poem, awarded the Mugen Prize, by Yoshimazu Gozo, earlier winner of the Takami Jun Prize. Japanese Poet in Residence, Oakland University, Fall 1979 and Winter 1980.

On cassette as performed simultaneously in Japanese and English by the poet and two contrasting voices with jazz improvization.

SUN, SAND AND WIND. Poems by Ben Shozu, one of the bolder young Japanese poets. Japanese Poet in Residence, Oakland University, Spring 1981.

PERSPECTIVES ON THE ARTS OF ASIA: JAPAN

THROUGH CLOSED DOORS: WESTERN INFLUENCE ON JAPANESE ART 1639-1853. Text by Cal French; 195 pp.; 157 plates. Published jointly by Meadow Brook Gallery of Art, Oakland University, and the Kobe City Museum of Namban Art, Kobe, Japan.

THE BANQUET AND THE SOLITARY MIND. Essays on Japanese poetry and culture by Ōoka Makoto, distinguished poet and critic.

Address inquiries and comments to the Editor, Thomas Fitzsimmons, Department of English, Oakland University, Rochester, MI 48063.